Charting New Waters
The Story Behind Success on The Spectrum

Nichole Daher

Dedication

To my stepdaughter,

You were the spark that lit this journey. Loving you opened my heart in ways I never expected, and you taught me more than any book, teacher, or coach ever could.

Though time and distance have grown between us, nothing can change the depth of my love for you or the impact you've had on the woman I became.

You were my greatest inspiration.

Acknowledgments

To Juliet—my right-hand man, my ride or die. Your hard work and loyalty are more valued than you will ever know. When I think back to the beginning, it feels like we were just babies chasing a dream. We've grown up together—learning, struggling, and thriving side by side. Now, we stand as strong, powerful women, and there is truly no one else I would have rather built this with.

To Kendra—the brains of the operation. I absolutely adore what we've created together. From day one, we've been in sync, building systems that just make sense. Your brilliance, passion, and intense knowledge have shaped the backbone of SOS. This company would not be what it is today without you.

To Joe—the one who believed, maybe even before I did, in how big SOS could become. You pushed me beyond my comfort zone and never let me settle for "good enough." Your vision helped me see the bigger picture, and your guidance has made a lasting impact—not just on the company but on who I am as a leader. Thank you for your trust, your hard work, and your unwavering support.

To Cathrine—the eyes of SOS, the windows to its soul. Without you, the world would never truly understand what SOS is capable of. Your life experiences, your wisdom, and your fierce heart came together to be exactly what this mission needed. In you, I gained more than a colleague—I gained a mother. Though you've endured unimaginable loss, you've poured that love into protecting this company and protecting me. Thank you for standing guard, for showing up, and for loving me so completely.

To Sabi—the heart and soul of SOS Franchising. The empath that we have grown to love with the "creeping" skills that we all admire. I have watched you grow from an insecure girl to a confident boss bitch. You always challenge me to see things from others' perspectives and offer a shoulder to cry on when my days are gray. Thank you for helping me build this empire.

About the Author

Nichole Daher is a stepmom, driving enthusiast, best-selling author, founder of *Success on the Spectrum*, and CEO of SOS Franchising.

Her journey began in 2015 when her small Autism Treatment Clinic opened and eventually evolved into a multiple 6-figure national franchise where she empowers aspiring entrepreneurs like YOU to embrace their destiny as business owners.

Whether you're an autism parent or not, you have the power to change the lives of thousands of families —and it all starts here.

Preface

People often admire the title "CEO," imagining corner offices, polished speeches, and big wins. But behind that title, there is often a story of sacrifice—quiet, painful, and deeply personal. This book is my story of becoming a successful CEO.

I didn't set out to become a business owner. I set out to help one little girl—my stepdaughter—access the support she deserved. I realized that autism treatment wasn't available in quantity or quality for her and the ever-growing number of kids in the autistic community. My want became a need to create something better, something lasting. What started as a simple mission to fill a gap in autism care grew into *Success on the Spectrum*, the first autism treatment franchise in the country.

As a CEO, I built clinics, created jobs, empowered entrepreneurs, and made therapy accessible for kids who were stuck in never-ending waitlists. I can sincerely say that I changed lives significantly and for the better, but in doing so, I lost parts of my own.

The more successful I became, the more my marriage fell apart. As the business rose, my relationship crumbled under the weight of ego, resentment, and the unsettling realization that sometimes, people love you more when you're small. The climb to the top came with a cost I never anticipated—loneliness in moments when there should have been partnership and silence where there should have been celebration.

This book is not just about building a company. It's about becoming a woman I never thought I'd be. It's about learning to lead while grieving, to grow while breaking, and to believe in a mission so deeply that I couldn't let it fail, even when everything else was falling apart.

If you've ever felt like your success came with a price, if you've ever chased a calling so loudly it drowned out the rest, or if you're standing at the edge wondering if you're brave enough to begin—this book is for you.

Contents

Chapter 1: Meet Your Captain

I come from a small town in Louisiana, where the hum of sugar cane plants and the rhythm of oil field shifts shaped the pulse of life. Every woman's expectations were simple and clear: marry a man who worked offshore or on the rigs, save every last dime until you can upgrade from a siding home to a brick home, and find contentment in weekends filled with standing around bonfires, drinking cheap beer, and listening to stories that never seemed to change.

While everyone else around me seemed so happy, I always felt like Belle from Beauty And The Beast. I craved something more exciting than my two-stoplight town could offer—something that didn't involve settling to fit the mold. I didn't want to live a boring life that had already been written for me. I felt like I didn't belong, that I was destined for a bigger life. I wanted to BE somebody—to do something that mattered. My ultimate fear was to die in the same town that I was born in.

I was never like the other girls in my town who dreamed of being stay-at-home moms, cooking casseroles, and cradling babies. The thought of pregnancy and childbirth made my skin crawl—I hated the idea of it. When I finally got the courage to say it out loud, my friends looked at me like I'd grown horns. They couldn't understand how anyone—especially a girl—could choose a career over starting a family. To them, it was selfish, ungrateful, fanciful even. The more I spoke my truth, the more they pulled away.

I felt like an outsider for wanting something different, for wanting more. Even through the loneliness, I knew I couldn't force myself into a life that wasn't mine.

My parents are not educated—my father never finished high school, and my mother dropped out of her first year of college when she got pregnant with me. However, they are both very entrepreneurial. My father started his own oil and gas business (as there is no other way to make money in Louisiana). My mother bought a small fitness franchise.

As you would expect, I was forced into "child labor" and worked for my mom. I actually liked working and the independence that the paycheck gave me. I was responsible, showed up on time, and completed all of my job duties well. The other staff there, even though they were older than me, would always look to me to make decisions in my mother's absence. I suppose they thought that the owner's daughter wouldn't get in trouble for making the wrong decision when an angry customer demanded a refund. I didn't appreciate it then, but I now know that it forced me to develop crisis management skills and leadership qualities.

I started planning my escape early, long before I had the means to actually leave. While other girls were buying makeup and Abercrombie jeans, I created a registry at Bed Bath & Beyond filled with dishes, toasters, and everything I'd need to live on my own. Every Christmas and birthday, I asked for housewares instead of trendy clothes or CDs. I knew that if I waited until I could afford everything on my own, it would take even longer to get out. My friends thought that I was weird.

By my junior year of high school, I had flipped through every career book on the shelves at Barnes & Noble, hungry for a path that felt like mine. That's when I found it—nuclear medicine. No one I knew had ever heard of it, which only made it more appealing. It was specialized, in-demand, and, most importantly, portable. I could work in any hospital, in any city, and live anywhere I wanted. It felt like my open ticket to the world—freedom disguised as a career. Once I decided, I went all in. I listed out my college classes down to the credit hour, calculating exactly how many I needed each semester to finish my degree as fast as possible. I wasn't just dreaming anymore—I was mapping my way out.

There weren't any colleges in Louisiana that offered a degree in nuclear medicine, so I enrolled in a virtual program through the University of Arkansas and carved my own path from behind a screen. In just four short years, I earned my bachelor's degree. It was the same year my little sister graduated high school, and by some twist of fate, both of our ceremonies landed on the same weekend. I didn't want to overshadow her moment—this was her time to shine—so I didn't tell my parents about my graduation. I let her have all the glory. I didn't need a cap and gown or applause to feel proud. I knew what I had accomplished, and that was enough for me.

I guess the local boys found it intriguing—maybe even refreshing—that I didn't want babies because, by the time I was 24, I'd already been engaged twice. Every boyfriend I had seemed eager to settle down, to lock in a life that felt suffocating to me. Every time the ring was on my finger, I couldn't bring myself to plan the wedding. The thought of being stuck in that small town felt more like a death sentence than a dream. It wasn't romantic. It was depressing.

My friends thought I was crazy—maybe even ungrateful—for walking away from "good men" who wanted to marry me. To them, I was throwing away the dream: a stable husband, a house, and kids. They couldn't wrap their heads around the fact that I didn't want that life— not because I was broken, but because I wanted something different. Some of them completely cut me off, like my choices were a threat to their own. They called me selfish, or stupid, or unrealistic. But deep down, I knew I wasn't running away—I was running toward something. Something bigger than what they could see from the edge of that small-town world.

After graduation, I started searching for jobs and landed one in Houston—the biggest city within a day's drive from my small hometown. It felt like the perfect first step into the life I'd always imagined.

My father wasn't happy about me moving away. He helped me load all the housewares I'd spent years collecting into a moving truck, but when it came time to hit the road, he refused to drive me there. Maybe it was a disappointment, maybe it was his way of trying to hold on—but I didn't let it shake me. I wasn't scared to drive anything, not even a massive UHaul. So off I went, behind the wheel and completely alone, heading toward my first apartment in the big city, finally ready to live out the dreams that had once seemed so far away.

When I arrived in Houston and stood in front of my new fifth-floor apartment, reality hit me hard—there was no way I could carry all those heavy boxes, mattresses, and furniture up five flights of stairs alone. But I wasn't about to let that stop me.

I did what any resourceful, determined woman would do: I headed to the nearest bar, had a couple of drinks, and turned on the charm. With a little confidence and my best social skills, I convinced a few friendly guys to come help me carry everything upstairs. It wasn't traditional, and it definitely wasn't planned, but it worked. Nothing—absolutely nothing—was going to get in the way of me building the life I dreamed of.

Chapter 2: Nichole in Love

I absolutely loved living in a big city. My downtown apartment felt like the center of the universe, with endless entertainment just steps from my front door. There was a park nearby where I'd walk my dog and catch outdoor movies under the stars—it felt like something out of a dream. Just down the street, a quirky little bar held turtle races every Wednesday night, and it quickly became one of my favorite oddball traditions. I'd spend weekends wandering through museums and getting lost in the dazzling maze of The Galleria shops. I witnessed the infamous Art Car Parade and watched my first Astros baseball game. The food scene was a whole new world—there were cuisines I'd never even heard of, and I wanted to try everything. Every corner held something new, and for the first time, life felt wide open and completely mine.

I started working at a small, unassuming diagnostic imaging clinic. I genuinely loved my work. I know it might sound strange, but my favorite part was starting IVs. There was something oddly satisfying about it, like a rare skill I had mastered. I thought it was so cool that I could slide a needle into a vein with such precision and ease. The radiation exposure never really scared me. While others worried about long-term risks, I shrugged it off. I never planned on having babies anyway, so that particular fear never stuck with me. I was finally doing what I set out to do, and that sense of purpose made everything worth it.

Once a week, I conducted nuclear stress tests. There was always a risk, a faint possibility, that the test might induce a heart attack in someone with pre-existing heart disease, and so a cardiologist had to be present, just in case.

My boss introduced me to the cardiologist who would be working alongside me. We shook hands, and our eyes met. And there he was—Mohammed Daher, a quadruple-boarded Lebanese doctor.

I didn't expect it, but he asked me on a date in the second week. I was flattered, but I wasn't stupid. Doctors, after all, had a reputation—players, they called them, men who thrived on the casual, the fleeting. He had just recently divorced his second wife (an ultrasound tech who also worked with us). It was the most scandalous gossip in the office. He was twelve years older than me and, honestly, gave off all the signs of a man deep in a midlife crisis. Dating him seemed like a bad idea, a guaranteed recipe for drama. But I was living this big, bold new life in the city, and part of me thought—why not? It may be the adventure I've been waiting for. It didn't have to be serious. Maybe it would be a mess. Maybe it would be fun. Either way, it felt like a story worth living.

I said yes—not immediately, but eventually. He picked me up for the first date in his BMW convertible. I remember the way the wind tangled my hair, the way the city lights blurred into streaks of gold. It felt like a dream, a moment suspended in time. We went to a sushi restaurant—already a luxury in my eyes. Without hesitation, he ordered two appetizers before the main course even arrived. To him, it was probably nothing. But for me, someone who grew up without much, appetizers and desserts were reserved for birthdays or rare celebrations. I remember feeling dubious, like he was throwing money at me, trying to impress me with extravagance. It was my first glimpse into our different upbringings.

Our second date was something truly special. He picked me up and told me he had a surprise planned. On the drive, he casually asked what my favorite food was, and without hesitation, I said pizza. To my surprise, he took me to a grocery store. We wandered the aisles hand in hand, laughing as we picked out all my favorite toppings. Back at his apartment, we created our pizza together and then popped it into the oven. Music played in the background as we danced around the kitchen, carefree and happy. At one point, we got into a playful argument about who sang "Boys of the Summer" and even made a bet on it. Turns out—we were both wrong… he still let me drive his convertible for a week as my prize.

As the dates continued, we grew closer, and the doubts began to fade. He was completely different than I expected. Unlike my modest upbringing, this man had grown up hopping across Europe and the Middle East—his childhood filled with experiences I had only read about. He was educated, worldly, and fluent in four languages. Compared to the Louisiana boys I had dated—the ones who rarely traveled beyond the state line—he was exotic. He was driven, ambitious, and in the process of launching his own private practice. It was intoxicating to be around someone with such vision, someone who had seen the world and wanted more from it. At the same time, it was intimidating. I wasn't used to being the one playing catch-up, but I was drawn to the challenge—and to him.

I don't think anyone in the world has ever pursued someone the way he pursued me. It was a whirlwind of romance straight out of a movie—hand-holding, picking me up from work for surprise lunch dates, deliveries of flowers and candy. He cleared out half of his master closet and insisted I leave my clothes at his house. I would always come back to my work scrubs being clean and pressed. He would make me breakfast and serve it to me on his balcony. We'd spend evenings on a beautiful outdoor patio, smoking hookah, sharing hummus, and talking for hours like the rest of the world had faded away. It didn't feel real. It felt like a dream I had somehow stepped into.

He whispered sweet nothings to me in French, his words soft and hypnotic. He gave me a tender Arabic nickname that made my heart flutter every time he said it.

When he took me to Lebanon to meet his parents, I was captivated. It was a breathtaking country where the mountains kissed the Mediterranean Sea, and the city pulsed with opulence and luxury. We visited places from his childhood, tucked between ancient beauty and modern glamour. His mother welcomed me instantly, her warmth wrapping around me like I belonged there all along.

I fell completely and utterly in love with him. I looked back at my friends, who had all settled for their small-town lives, with a smile. I'd always known this was waiting for me. I wasn't crazy.

I was curious about his past—two divorces weren't something you could just ignore—so I asked him one night, gently, about his previous marriages. He laughed, a little too casually, and said it seemed like his life happened in "8-year cycles". He told me he had been with his first wife for eight years before cheating on her with the woman who became his second wife. He admitted it with a mix of guilt and reflection, saying he regretted how he handled it, that he should have just left instead of breaking her heart that way. His relationship with the second wife also lasted eight years. He claimed he never truly wanted to marry her, but he wasn't yet a citizen and feared losing custody or rights to see his daughter. According to him, she used that fear against him— always threatening to take his child away unless he bought her something or gave in to her demands. They were only legally married for a few months before he filed for divorce. It was a messy, complicated story— one that made me pause, even as I sat there wrapped in the glow of a romance that felt like magic.

Mohammed assured me that our relationship was different. With the kind of beautiful, poetic words that made your heart believe even when your mind had questions, he told me he had never felt this way about anyone before. He said I saw the real him— the parts no one else had ever bothered to look for. He swore our love was eternal, something rare and destined. He called me his "winged goddess," a name that made me feel both powerful and cherished like I was the light that lifted him above the wreckage of his past. It was intoxicating to be adored like that.

Chapter 3: Becoming a Mother

Mohammed introduced me to his children. Two girls, one from each marriage, both beautiful in their own ways. The oldest, Lilo, was nine years old, her dark eyes like pools of ink, brown skin, and her hair encompassed beautiful tales of curls. The youngest, Meez, was five, her eyes a startling blue, like shards of sky caught in a frame of dark, pale white skin, and dark curly hair. She had autism, and there was a fragility to her that made my heart ache.

We met at the park that played outdoor movies that I frequented, where the scent of grass and popcorn helped ease what could have been an awkward situation. I brought them gifts— glow-in-the-dark glasses. The girls were shy at first, their eyes darting to me, then to their father, then back to me. He introduced me as "Daddy's friend," a cautious label, a test of sorts. The youngest smiled, her curiosity piqued. "Do you want to sit by me?" she asked in a voice that was soft and tentative, and so I did. During the scary parts of the movie, her small hand found mine, her grip tight, trusting. They both watched the screen with wide eyes, their glow-in-the-dark glasses casting a faint, otherworldly light on their faces.

Meez was a gorgeous child, truly, but it wasn't just her looks that captivated me; it was her sweetness, her cuddliness, and the way she curled into me as though I were a safe harbor in a storm. "Oh, God," I remember thinking, "she's adorable." And she absolutely was.

I never wanted to have babies. But this—this was different. This was a win-win, as I saw it. I got to skip the sleepless nights, the diapers, and the grinding demands of infancy. Instead, I stepped into a world of giggles, bedtime stories, and the excitement of Christmas morning. It was the good stuff, the sweet stuff, and I reveled in it. It was everything that I never knew I wanted.

My mom was always supportive of my new family. She was excited that I finally had a child. She went around town telling all of her friends that she had a granddaughter who was "artistic." I just rolled my eyes and eventually stopped correcting her.

But not everyone was happy for me. Some of my friends were concerned; their voices showed worry when they asked how I felt about taking on the responsibility of a stepchild— a child with special needs, no less. They knew I had never wanted children of my own and had never felt the pull of motherhood in the way so many others did. They worried that I would feel trapped and that the relationship wouldn't work out because of the weight of his responsibilities. Even strangers made uninvited comments to me, like, "I would never raise another woman's child."

But I didn't feel trapped. I didn't feel burdened. If anything, I felt the opposite. Being a stepmother to her wasn't work; it was a joy. It fulfilled me in ways I hadn't anticipated and gave me a sense of purpose that I hadn't known I was missing.

I didn't define myself as a mother—not in the way some people do, as though it were the core of their identity—but I loved it. I loved her, and I was good at it. I took pride in that, in the life I was able to give her, in the stability and love I could provide.

Meez's biological mother, on the other hand, was absent. She had other children with several other men, none of whom she had custody of. She didn't enjoy being a mother and didn't seem to find any fulfillment in it. Yet she kept having babies, only to abandon them. While I didn't judge her—not really—I couldn't help but feel a sense of pride in the fact that I was able to give Meez the stability that her biological mother couldn't. It wasn't about being better; it was about being there, about showing up, day after day, in the ways that mattered.

By the sixth month of dating, Mohammed left a sticky note on my desk at work. A simple request, scrawled in his hurried handwriting: *Move in with me.* I was so surprised I actually screamed out loud. My office manager heard and poked her head in my room. I showed the note to her and we both hopped up and down in excitement while screaming together like a couple of young girls.

The timing was perfect—my lease was ending, and the idea of building a life together, of stepping into this ready-made family, felt like the natural next step. So I agreed. I packed up my apartment and moved into his to start a life together.

Mohammad constantly showered me with compliments about how good I was to his children. He told me, over and over, how grateful he was that I treated them with love and kindness. Meez's mother hadn't treated Lilo well, and that lingering fear—that history might repeat itself—was something he carried with him. After the girls returned from spending Mother's Day away, he made sure I felt seen and appreciated. He had them color a sweet little card and sign it. He bought me simple but thoughtful gifts—nothing flashy, but meaningful. It felt like love in its purest, most sincere form.

One day, Mohammed picked me up from work and said that he had a surprise. He drove us to a car dealership. Range Rover. I looked at him with shock. He shrugged, "I can't have you driving my kids around in that Scion tC. It's got over 200,000 miles on it. You're gonna break down any minute."

He walked over to an SUV that had already been washed and parked out front. "You like it?" I couldn't even speak. I half thought he was joking. I looked around for the hidden cameras—but there were none. We took pictures next to it, and he threw me the keys. I felt like I was living in a dream.

A few months later, Mohammed told me that he wanted to marry me. I could not have been happier. It was fast, but I felt sure about him. I had centered my whole life around him and the kids already, why not make it official?

I shopped around for the ring I wanted—looking for a unique diamond. I found a 2.5-carat Asscher that called to me. He unexpectedly shoved thousands of dollars of cash into my hand and told me to go get it. I was shocked and even more happy.

We planned a small Vegas wedding and bought matching dresses for the girls. Meez was so excited to be the flower girl, and Lilo giggled when I asked her to be the ring bearer. They practiced in our living room while I laughed.

The ceremony was quick and easy. Our closest family attended—my mom and Mohammed's youngest brother signed as witnesses on our marriage certificate. We took beautiful pictures together and had champagne with our friends. Mohammed surprised me with a beautiful letter "to his wife," listing out all the reasons why he loved me. I read it out loud in front of everyone. I cried, my friends cried, my mom cried. It was the best day of my life.

Back at home, Mohammed's practice was busy—always busy. His schedule was packed with appointments and emergencies, and he relied on a nanny to manage Meez's therapy sessions, her doctor's visits, and the endless logistics of her care. But not long after I moved in, the nanny quit. She moved away, leaving a void that I instinctively stepped into. My job was flexible; his wasn't. It made sense, as a couple, to tackle these things together. And so I became her primary mode of transportation, shuttling her to and from ABA therapy, packing her lunches, and picking out her clothes. I embraced it all: the mommy things, the small, daily acts of love that wove us together.

But living with this child wasn't always easy. It was here, in the quiet chaos of our shared life, that I got a real taste of what autism was. Meez was not a morning person. Waking her up was an art that required precision and patience. If you got it wrong—if you nudged her too gently or too abruptly— the consequences were immediate and devastating. Her tantrums were not the tantrums of a neurotypical child (the term neurotypical, I learned, is used for anyone who is "normal"). They were something else entirely, something primal and raw.

It was as if her brain had misfired, as if some ancient survival instinct had been triggered. She would scream, kick, bite, and cry—her small body convulsing with a force that seemed far too great for her frame. It was a full-blown fight- or-flight sympathetic response; her body convinced, on some deep, unshakable level, that she was fighting for her life. And there was nothing you could do to calm her. Nothing. You could only wait, your heart breaking as you watched her struggle, as you listened to her cries echo through the apartment. It was traumatic for her and for me.

Even in those moments, even when I felt utterly helpless, I loved her. I loved her fiercely, unconditionally. She was my stepdaughter, my unexpected gift, and I would have done anything for her. Mohammed was better at it than I was— calming her down, de-escalating the storms that seemed to rise out of nowhere. There was a quiet mastery in the way he handled her, a patience that I envied and admired in equal measure. But I couldn't always rely on him. I needed to learn, to understand, to become better at knowing the tempest of her emotions. So, I began to take parent training classes at her ABA therapy center. It was there that I began to comprehend the power of behavior modification. I also didn't realize how much of my own understanding of parenting would have to change to meet her where she was.

Before I began my journey as a stepmother, my understanding of autism was limited, shaped by stereotypes and misconceptions that I didn't even realize I carried. In my mind, autism was something severe, something obvious—a child who drooled, who flapped their hands, who couldn't speak or function in the world. I didn't know that autism could look different, that it could be subtle, nuanced, and hidden behind a mask of high intelligence and social adaptation.

I didn't know, for example, that Mohammed was autistic. Not at first. He was brilliant, had the memory retention of an elephant, and was deeply knowledgeable about his favorite subjects. I loved how differently his brain worked, like he thought in 3D. But he didn't have many friends, and I had always assumed that was because he was busy, because his work consumed him. He had hobbies, yes, but I didn't see them as obsessions—just passions, the way anyone might have a favorite pastime. It wasn't until I began taking these ABA parenting classes and reading books about autism that I started to recognize these traits in him.

The way he struggled with social cues, the way he fixated on certain topics, the way he needed routine and structure to feel secure. He had never been formally diagnosed—autism wasn't something that was widely recognized or understood in the '70s, especially in Europe—but it was clear to me now. He was high-functioning, yes, but he was autistic. I think that knowledge helped me communicate better with him.

It also helped me understand my stepdaughter better. Her development had been different from what I had expected. Most children follow a predictable progression when learning to speak—babbling first, then single words, then sentences. But she didn't follow that path. She went from not talking at all to speaking in full, complex sentences as though she had been storing up words inside her, waiting for the right moment to release them. I remember joking about it one day with my mother-in-law, and she laughed. "Oh, Mohammed did the same thing," she said with a wave of her hand. And in that moment, it clicked: *of course*, I thought, *it's genetic.*

As I grew more familiar with autism, I began to see it everywhere in my husband's family—it was subtle but unmistakable once you knew what to look for. His brother had it—quiet, reserved, with a mind that could unravel complex problems but struggled with small talk. His father had it, too, though his was more pronounced. He was a brilliant political speaker and a lawyer with a mind like a steel trap, able to recite the Geneva Convention verbatim from memory, but he could not operate a microwave. He could talk for hours about history, about law, about the books he had read, but ask him how his day was, and he would just shrug. It was fascinating, in a way, to see how these men had lived through the world, high-functioning enough to slide by unnoticed, their autism hidden beneath layers of intellect and achievement. And now, knowing what I knew, I couldn't unsee it. *Oh my God*, I thought. *It's everywhere in this family.*

I learned about the functions of behavior and how to identify the triggers that set off the fight-or-flight reflex in her brain. I learned to recognize the subtle signs that preceded a tantrum: the way her body tensed, the way her breathing quickened, the way her eyes darted as though searching for an escape. It was like learning a new language, one that allowed me to see the world through her eyes, to understand the chaos that sometimes overwhelmed her. And it all began to make sense. It all clicked.

Coincidentally, in college, I had taken developmental psychology classes. They were ancillary courses, something to fill the humanities requirement, but they had lingered in the back of my mind, fragments of knowledge that now came rushing forward. The theories, the studies, the case histories—they all connected with what I was learning now. It was as though the pieces of a puzzle were falling into place, revealing a picture I hadn't known I was trying to solve.

I discovered that ABA therapy was practical and grounded in the here and now. It wasn't the kind of therapy where someone sits in a chair and recounts the traumas of their childhood, searching for answers in the past. No, this was different. This was about action, about recognizing the function of a behavior in the moment and applying an intervention to change the outcome. It was about understanding why she did what she did and finding ways to guide her toward better choices, and to me, it was glorious. It was like watching a machine come to life, each part working in harmony to create something beautiful.

I devoured books on autism and the ways to help children recognize their own triggers and apply their own self-control. I wanted to understand her, to help her, to give her the tools she needed to live in this world that often felt too loud, too bright, too much. And as I learned, I began to see changes—not just in her, but in myself. The way I approached parenting and the way I reacted to situations began to change. My own upbringing had been different. The way my parents had raised me was not the way I wanted to raise her. Their methods were rooted in punishment—as a consequence of bad behavior.

With an autistic child, punishment doesn't work. It only teaches them to avoid the punishment, not to desire the "right" behavior. Instead, ABA therapy taught me to reward the good, to ignore the bad, to focus on reinforcing the behaviors I wanted to see. It was a different way of thinking, a different way of being, and it was hard. Old habits, after all, die hard. The instincts I had inherited from my own rearing were hard to unlearn, but I was determined.

I began to see the world in a new light, to understand that her tantrums were not acts of defiance but cries for help, signals that she was overwhelmed, that she needed support. And I began to see the beauty in the small victories—the moments when she calmed herself, recognized her own triggers, and found ways to cope. It was slow, painstaking work, but it was worth it.

Now, I was no longer just a stepmother, a stand-in for a role I had never imagined myself in. I was her advocate, her guide, and her safe place, and though the journey was difficult, I wouldn't have traded it for anything. She had changed me, this gorgeous, cuddly, complicated child. She had taught me patience and empathy.

To me, ABA therapy was more than just a method; it became a philosophy, a way of seeing the world. It was common sense, rooted in its simplicity. Reward the good, ignore the bad. Encourage the behaviors you want to see, and let the rest fade away. I fell in love with it, with the clarity it brought, the way it made sense of the chaos.

And Meez—she was thriving. From the time I met her at five years old until she turned seven, the changes were remarkable. She became more verbal, her words spilling out in hesitant but determined bursts. She made more eye contact, her gaze meeting mine with a connection that felt like a small miracle. And then there was the food.

For the first six years of her life, her diet had been painfully restrictive: Caesar salad and hot dogs. That was it. Her ABA therapy center introduced a food program, turning the act of trying new foods into a game, a fun activity, rather than a battle.

One day, at a sushi restaurant, she surprised us all. Trying to encourage independence skills, we prompted Meez to talk to the waitress and order her own food. "I want a Caesar salad with all of the things I like and none of the things I don't like," she instructed matter-of-factly. The waitress looked at me for help. I laughed so hard that my sides hurt. She was so darn cute. Mohammed ordered a peppered tuna appetizer.

When the tuna arrived, she looked at it, her eyes wide with curiosity. "I want some," she said. Mohammed and I exchanged a glance. Raw sushi wasn't exactly kid food, but we were so thrilled that she wanted to try something new that we couldn't say no. She ate the whole thing, her small face lighting up with each bite. We ended up ordering two more servings, our excitement bubbling over. It wasn't just about the food—it was about what it represented. Progress. Growth. A willingness to step outside the narrow boundaries of her comfort zone.

The tantrums didn't disappear—they were still there, still intense, still heartbreaking—but they became less frequent. And her thinking, once driven by gut reactions, began to shift. She started to reason, to connect actions with consequences, to make decisions based on logic rather than impulse. It was incredible to witness this blossoming of her mind, this slow unfurling of her potential.

It wasn't all smooth sailing. There were moments that tested me, stretched me thin, and left me raw. One of the hardest things was the disconnect between what I had loved as a child and what she enjoyed. I would watch her at the park or at summer camp, surrounded by children her age, and see how they excluded her, how they left her out of their games, their laughter, their secret worlds. It broke my heart. I wanted so badly for her to belong, to be included, to feel the joy of friendship that I had taken for granted as a child. But it wasn't that simple.

The other children didn't understand her, and she didn't always understand them. They moved in different rhythms and had far more social skills, and the gap between them felt impossibly wide.

One day, it all came to a head. There was a birthday party—a classmate's celebration—and every girl in the group was invited except her. I saw the invitations being handed out, saw the excitement on the other children's faces, and felt the sting of exclusion as though it were my own. I couldn't bear it and had a little tantrum of my own. I confronted the mother in the parking lot, my anger spilling out in a torrent of words.

"I hope you're happy," I said, my voice trembling with fury. "You're teaching your child to discriminate. You're teaching her that it's okay to leave out the special needs kid. And *you're* the adult. You're the one setting the example. So congratulations—you're Mom of the Year."

I didn't care that other parents were watching, that I was making a scene. At that moment, all I cared about was her— my child, my stepdaughter, this beautiful, innocent girl who deserved so much more than the world was giving her. I wanted to shield her from the cruelty of exclusion, to wrap her in a bubble of love and acceptance, but I couldn't. All I could do was stand up for her, even if it meant standing alone.

I knew I had crossed a line, that my outburst might have made things worse. But I was absolutely not capable of staying silent. Her worth, her dignity, her right to be included— those things mattered. And if no one else would fight for her, then I would. Meez was my child in every way that mattered, and I would do whatever it took to give her the life she deserved.

Years later, when she was grown, I told a friend about that parking lot confrontation. I recounted it with a kind of pride, the way we sometimes do when we look back on moments where we stood up for what we believed was right. But Meez, who was eavesdropping, looked at me with a quiet, knowing expression. "I didn't even want to go to that party," she said. Her words were simple, but they hit me like a thunderclap. "I hate birthday parties. They are stressful. I don't like them."

All those years ago, I had been fighting for her to be included, to be invited, to be part of the social activity that I remembered so fondly from my own childhood. But for her, that world wasn't a source of joy—it was a source of discomfort, of overwhelm. I had been fighting for the wrong things, projecting my own nostalgia onto her, trying to give her the childhood I thought she should have rather than the one she actually wanted.

It was a mind-blowing realization that forced me to confront the ways in which I had misunderstood her, the ways in which I had let my own expectations cloud my judgment. Becoming a parent—a stepparent—had required me to change not just the way I thought but the way I defined what a good childhood looked like. Her definition of happiness was not the same as mine, and it was my job to learn that, to honor it, to let go of my own preconceptions and meet her where she was.

Even then, I didn't feel burdened by it, scared or worried. For me, it was never a question of whether I could handle it; it was simply a fact of life, a part of the man I loved and the family we were building together.

There was a day early in my journey as a stepparent that I couldn't ever forget—not because it was joyful, but because it was raw, unfiltered, and painfully real. It was a day that highlighted both the struggles and the complexities of loving a child with autism, a day that tested me in ways I hadn't expected.

I had picked her up from ABA therapy—what we called "school"—and we were driving home. The drive was long, about an hour, and the car was quiet at first, but then she spoke, her voice small but insistent. "Can we go back to the store and get the toy I want?" she asked.

The day before, I had taken her to a store and told her she could pick out one item. She had found two things she wanted, and I had made her a deal: if she had a good day at school the next day, we would go back and get the second item. But that day had not been a good one. She had struggled—a tantrum in the classroom, an attempt to hit another student. The note from her teacher, handed to me at pickup, had made that clear. And so, when she asked about the store, I reminded her of our agreement. "You didn't have a good day today," I said gently. "You weren't nice to your friend in class. So we're not going to go to the store today. But you can try again tomorrow. If you do well tomorrow, I'll take you then."

Her response was immediate, her voice rising in panic. "But what if it's not there tomorrow? What if someone buys all of them?"

I tried to reassure her. "It's still going to be there. And if it's not, we'll go to another store and find it." But my words didn't calm her. Instead, they seemed to ignite something in her, a storm of frustration and fear that she couldn't contain.

The tantrum began quietly at first, a low whine that quickly escalated into screams. And then, as I drove, she unbuckled her seatbelt. I heard the click and the rustle of movement, and then her small hands were on me, hitting my shoulders and my arms. I yelled, my voice sharp with alarm. "Get back! You're going to cause an accident! This is dangerous!" But she didn't stop. She slid down in her seat, her feet kicking toward me, aiming for my head. The Range

Rover swerved slightly as I tried to maintain control, my heart pounding in my chest.

I pulled over, my hands trembling on the wheel, and got out of the car. I opened the back door and pulled her out, my voice firm but shaking. "You cannot do that!" I said, my words measured, my breath uneven. "You cannot unbuckle yourself. You cannot hit me. You cannot kick me. It's not safe." Out of my own instinctive reaction, I spanked her for the first (and last) time.

She was crying now, her face red and streaked with tears, her body rigid with anger and fear. I stood there on the side of the road, emotionally struggling, feeling utterly helpless. What do you do in a moment like that? How do you reach a child who is so overwhelmed, so lost in their own emotions, that they can't see the danger, can't hear your voice, can't see anything but their own desire?

It was a terrible experience, one that left me shaken and exhausted. It was also a reminder—a stark, unflinching reminder—of the challenges we faced. Loving her wasn't always easy. It wasn't always the picture-perfect moments of connection and joy that I had imagined. It was messy, complicated, and sometimes heartbreaking. But it was also real. And in those moments, as hard as they were, I learned something about myself, about her, about the kind of love that doesn't give up, even when it's hard.

I had to keep reminding myself of the rules of ABA therapy: "Don't punish the behavior. Reward the good. Ignore the bad." But how could I ignore this? How could I let something so dangerous, so overwhelming, go without consequence? And yet, I knew that punishing her wouldn't work. It would only teach her to avoid the punishment, not to understand why her actions were wrong. So I stood there on the edge of the highway, holding her as she screamed and kicked, waiting for the storm to pass. It took an hour—an hour of tears, of frustration, of trying to appeal to her logic when logic was the last thing on her mind. And when it was over, when she finally slumped against me, exhausted and spent, I felt a doubt crash over me. What am I doing? I thought. I can't handle this. We're going to die on the highway. I'm going to wreck this car. I'm not cut out for this. It was one of the hardest moments of my life, a moment that made me question everything.

But then there were the good moments, the ones that made it all worth it. Meez was a nerd in the best possible way. She loved knowledge, loved facts, loved the kind of books that most kids would find boring. She would sit for hours, flipping through the dictionary or reading science fact books, her face lit up with curiosity and wonder. And so, for her birthday, I decided to throw her a science-themed party. It was my way of celebrating her, of showing her that her passions mattered, that she mattered.

I hired a mad scientist-themed company to come to our house. They set up in the backyard, their tables cluttered with beakers and test tubes, their voices full of theatrical excitement. They made a volcano that erupted in a cascade of foam and mixed chemicals that bubbled and fizzed. The kids made slime—bright, gooey, and utterly irresistible. I had t-shirts printed for the occasion, each one emblazoned with "Meez's Mad Scientist Birthday Party" and a cut out of her face on a little cartoon scientist's body. She and I dressed matching in white lab coats, our hair in pigtails, our faces framed by oversized lab goggles. We even wore the same lip gloss, a small, silly detail that made her giggle with delight.

When she saw the setup, her eyes widened, and she looked at me as though I had hung the moon. "This is the best birthday party ever," she said, her voice filled with awe. "Thank you so much. I love you so much." It was a win, a bright, shining win in a journey that was often met with challenges.

It wasn't just her reaction that made me happy. It was the fact that people showed up. Some of my friends brought their kids, and even though they weren't from her therapy class, they were kids she knew, kids who played with her and laughed with her, and made her feel included. For once, the backyard was full—full of laughter, cake on paper plates, and balloons. It was the kind of chaos that only a group of happy, excited children can create. And I felt it then, that rare, fleeting sense of triumph. *Yes*, I thought. *I did it right. I did something right.* I felt like I had finally hit my stride as a stepmother. I was "supermom," as I liked to call myself, in those moments of quiet pride.

She was socially awkward around groups of her peers but wasn't shy in front of a camera. She loved watching YouTube videos, so one day, I suggested we make our own.

"Let's start a cooking show," I said, and her face lit up with excitement. And so we did. We created a little channel just for us and filmed ourselves making brownies and cookies. It wasn't fancy—we used boxed mixes, the kind where you just add milk and stir—but it was ours.

I would set up the camera, and she would stand in front of it, her pigtails bouncing as she announced, "Welcome, guys, to my cooking show! Today, we're making cookies!" She would pour the mix into the bowl, her small hands gripping the spoon as she stirred, her face serious with concentration. And then, halfway through, she would turn to me and whisper, "I need help putting this in the oven." She knew the rules—the oven was hot, and she couldn't touch it. So I would stop the camera, slide the tray into the oven, and then start filming again as she declared, "Now you let it bake for 15 minutes! Don't forget to like and subscribe to my channel!"

Those videos were precious to me, little snapshots of a time when it was just the two of us laughing and creating together.

I always giggled at her nuances. Her motor function was such a mixed bag. It took months for her to learn how to open a door—she struggled with pushing the handle while twisting the knob at the same time. We spent years teaching her to tie shoelaces. I think I got carpal tunnel from trying to teach her to ride a bike without training wheels, which she never grasped. But the first time she put on snow skis, she was like a fish to water. Who would have guessed that this would be her hidden talent?

Like any parent, there were days when I felt lost, when I questioned whether I was doing enough, whether I was giving her the life she deserved. But there were also moments of clarity, moments when I saw her thriving in her own way, on her own terms. And those moments reminded me that love isn't about forcing someone into a mold—it's about meeting them where they are, about celebrating who they are, not who you think they should be.

As much as the ABA therapy center helped her, there was always the knowledge that it wouldn't last forever. When we learned that she would age out of the program, I felt panicked. On one hand, I was proud of how far she had come, of the strides she had made. On the other, I was terrified. What would happen next? Where would she go? The therapy center had been a great help not just for her but for me. It had given me the tools I needed to help her, understand her, and understand the complexities of her world. And now, that support was being taken away.

It was a hard pill to swallow. She wasn't ready. I knew this in the marrow of my bones, in the way a mother knows her child's breathing, her rhythms, her silences. She wasn't ready, and yet the world was insisting, pulling her toward something she could not yet bear.

The tantrums still came, sharp and unrelenting, born not of mischief but of something deeper, something instinctual, something that logic could not reach. And then there was the running—the eloping, they called it, a delicate word for something that felt like terror. If she did not like what was said, what was asked of her, she would flee. A door left ajar; a moment's distraction and she would be gone.

In a public school classroom of twenty kids, who would run after her? Who would leave the others behind to follow her small body as it disappeared down a hallway, out a door, into the chaos beyond? Would she find herself in the parking lot, cars moving, doors swinging open and shut, the world oblivious to her presence? Would she be seen? Would she be safe?

The thought of it consumed me. I saw the progress we had built, brick by careful brick, and I saw it crumbling in an instant—one wrong step, one unfamiliar hand trying to restrain her, one misunderstanding that spiraled too far. Without the therapists, without the ones who knew her, who understood what autism meant beyond a textbook definition, what would happen to her?

She wasn't ready. And so, I searched. I combed through every ABA center and every program that might take a child over seven years old, but there were so few. Houston, the medical capital of the world, was a city bursting with hospitals and specialists, yet the doors for children like mine were nearly all shut. The places that did exist held waiting lists so long they stretched into uncertainty—six months, a year, and even then, no promises. I toured one place that claimed it accepted older children, but when I stepped inside, I saw the truth. The play equipment was small and built for toddlers. The children there were tiny and unknowing, no older than five. I searched the rooms, hoping, willing another seven-year-old into existence, but there were none.

At the final clinic that I toured, the owner asked, "How old is she?" her voice all business.

"Seven," I said, and I saw it in her eyes before she spoke, the quiet dismissal, the certainty of rejection.

"She'll never get approved," she told me, flat and final. "You should just give that up and put her in school."

Give up!?! That night, I went home, anger threading through my teeth as I told my husband what that awful woman had said. "Give up" as if those words could ever belong to a mother. As if I could ever look at my stepdaughter and let the world decide she was not worth fighting for.

And then he laughed. Not unkindly, not dismissively, but with humor. "Well," he said, "if all these places have waitlists, business must be good. You should open one of your own."

It was a joke. A passing thought, but it landed somewhere deep inside me, settled in my chest, and took root. Maybe I will. Maybe I will build the thing they say cannot exist. Maybe I will open the biggest, strongest, most unshakable clinic, one that does not turn children away because they have lived too many years, one that does not tell mothers to give up. Maybe I will prove that woman wrong.

I'm not saying that I opened a business out of spite—though if I am honest, it felt so good to prove her wrong.

Chapter 4: The Birth of SOS

The idea of starting my own ABA company was more than just appealing—it was empowering. I had experienced rejection from so many ABA therapy facilities, and I was tired of feeling helpless. I wanted more for her. I wanted consistency, quality, and a place where she would always be welcomed. Starting my own clinic felt like the answer. As a business owner, I could make my own hours, set my own standards, and finally take control of the care Meez deserved.

There was just one small problem: I had never owned a business before. To make things more complicated, I had zero experience in the field of Applied Behavior Analysis. What I did have was a stubborn belief that I could figure it out. I believed I could work harder than anyone else and surround myself with people who knew what I didn't. I was fully prepared to learn everything that couldn't be found in books.

So I started where anyone would—I picked up the phone. I knew that the ABA therapy company that had just "graduated" Meez had a solid foundation. They had a long waitlist, and the business seemed to be thriving. I thought, why not partner with someone who's already built what I hope to create? I called and asked for the owner, over and over, until I finally got her on the line.

When she answered, I launched into the best version of my carefully practiced pitch. I offered to open a second location on the other side of town. I explained how it made perfect sense to grow her brand, reach more families, and turn her success into something bigger. All I asked in return was for her to teach me how to run the clinic—we would make the perfect partners.

What I got in response was one of the most astonishing displays of disinterest I'd ever encountered. She wasn't just uninterested—she was completely checked out. She told me she no longer enjoyed working in ABA, rarely stepped foot in her clinic, and had no intention of expanding. I pivoted, offering to buy the company outright. She said that she was already in the process of a sale and that I wouldn't be able to afford it anyway. I begged her to franchise—promised to open my own clinic under her brand and pay royalties if she would just guide me through the process.

She laughed, almost condescendingly, and said, "Oh honey, franchising a business costs hundreds of thousands of dollars. And I wouldn't want to do that much work anyway."

I hung up that call feeling underestimated, dismissed, and more fired up than ever. Maybe I was only 28 years old. Maybe I didn't have the experience or the fancy business degree. But what I did have was a reason. A very personal one. And I was just getting started.

Later, I searched for the numbers to see if she was telling the truth—it really does cost one hundred to two hundred thousand dollars to convert a business into a franchise. The weight of it was crushing, a sum so colossal it seemed to stretch into the ceiling of the world. My shoulders sagged beneath its imagined gravity. Fine, I thought. I'd find an ABA center that is already a franchise and join. Someone must have already thought of this. Surely.

But there was nothing. It was a hollow field of silence. No paths. No maps. No signs. Just a great, dry expanse and the sense that if anything was to be built, I would have to do it with my own bare hands, but I hardly knew anything at all.

So I did what I could—I read. Books became my companions, and Google was my whispering mentor; at three a.m. I pieced together a plan, clumsy and half-believed, built on late-night estimations and intuition. I looked at all of Meez's old therapy bills and turned them into a blueprint. I noted what our health insurance had paid, how much behavior technicians earned, and what behavior analysts cost to oversee treatment, to train, to hold it all together.

One child wouldn't be enough. I knew that immediately. To afford even a single analyst, I would need more kids to make the numbers work. I envisioned Meez and about three other kids. I could clear out my formal dining room (we never ate at home anyway) and put in little desks and a cute chalkboard. I imagined singing and laughter echoing through the house. It would be perfect.

So, I crafted a message and sent it fluttering into the world. I posted in the Autism Moms Facebook group, a place pulsing with shared exhaustion. I wrote: "I'm hiring a behavior analyst. I'm tired of waiting lists and the lack of clinics that don't serve children over seven. If I hire these people to come to my house, who wants in?"

The response was overwhelming. Dozens of replies. *Yes. Interested. Me too.* There popped up tons of mothers, all aching for the same thing. In no time, thirty families reached out. And I knew I could make this work.

When I told my husband I was going for it, he looked at me with surprise. I don't think he actually believed I would do it—not really. He listened patiently as I described my vision, nodding here and there, but I could tell it was more to humor me than anything else. I don't blame him. I'd never started a business before. I didn't have a background in ABA. I didn't have an MBA. From the outside, it probably sounded like some big idea that would fizzle out with time.

He asked broad questions about how I would do it. He was worried about people coming into our home. He played it down as liability, but I knew it was social anxiety. He wouldn't want to talk to anyone coming or going.

"How are you going to afford to start this up?" I told him I had good credit and planned to get a loan. I pulled out my amateur business plan—as a Type A personality, I love a good spreadsheet—and walked him through how the numbers seemed to make sense. He lifted his eyebrows, a little impressed.

That night, we went out to a small Mexican restaurant. We sat outside on the patio, me feeling the excitement of possibility. Between bites of chips and salsa, we kept talking about the business. What would we name it? I told him I wanted something obvious. A name that said exactly what we did—no guessing, no vague branding. It had to include the word "spectrum" because I wanted families like mine to know right away that we were here for them.

I scribbled a list of ideas onto a paper napkin, crossing out the ones that sounded too stiff, too sterile, or too unclear. Then Mohammed said out loud: "Succeed on the Spectrum." We both paused, smiled, and repeated it. It was a bit of a mouthful, sure, but it said everything we needed it to say. And the tagline? That part came easy: We help children succeed on the spectrum. It felt right.

Excited, I pulled out my phone and quickly typed in the URL www.succeedonthespectrum.com. Taken. I groaned— but only for a moment. So I pivoted. I searched again, fingers trembling slightly on the keyboard.

www.successonthespectrum.com — available! And just like that, the name was born. *Success on the Spectrum.* Naming it made it real. It felt like I had willed it into the universe: I will make this happen. There will be success. There will be hope.

Over the next few weeks, I started making a list of everything I'd need to launch the business—licenses, staffing, insurance, equipment, legal paperwork, and about a hundred other things I had never dealt with before. I was learning everything from scratch, googling one term after another, piecing it all together like a giant, unfamiliar puzzle.

I did a lot of my research at work. Nuclear scans could take hours, and during the long, quiet stretches of downtime, I'd sneak over to the office computer and dive into my next question. How do I start an LLC? How do I buy a website domain? How do you hire a BCBA? What insurance companies cover ABA therapy? How do I get in the network? It felt like I was living a double life—Nuclear Medicine Tech by day and an aspiring entrepreneur by... also day. But I was determined.

Sean, my office bestie, started noticing how often I was glued to the screen with tabs open that had nothing to do with radiology. He raised an eyebrow one day and said, "Okay... what are you up to?" So I told him. All of it.

He didn't laugh. He didn't act surprised. He leaned in, asked questions, and started throwing out ideas with me. I honestly think Sean was the only person who fully believed I was really going to do it. Everyone else smiled politely or nodded vaguely. But Sean? He looked me dead in the eye and said, "You're actually going to pull this off, aren't you?" I just smiled. Because deep down, I knew he was right.

I shopped around at several banks, trying to secure a business loan. I was optimistic at first—confident that with good credit and a solid plan, I'd be approved. But reality hit hard. I was denied every SBA startup loan I applied for because Mohammad wasn't a US citizen. That detail, which had never mattered in our day-to-day lives, suddenly became a massive roadblock.

So, I pivoted and tried to apply for a traditional business loan instead. Again, I was shut down—this time because of Mohammad's credit. His divorce from Meez's mother had left his credit history in rough shape, and even though I was the one building the business, it still counted against me.

I could see the frustration on his face. I think he felt bad—maybe even embarrassed—that he was the reason I kept hitting dead ends. So, one evening, he quietly offered me $60,000 from his personal savings. I was stunned. Grateful didn't even begin to cover it. That money wasn't just financial support—it was belief. It was a gesture that said, Okay... maybe you really are going to do this. And it lit a fire in me. I was motivated before, but now I was unstoppable. I wasn't just building a business anymore—I was proving that his sacrifice, his faith in me, wasn't misplaced.

At some point in the journey, I started shortening the business name, *Success on the Spectrum*, to just "SOS." It felt natural—catchy, memorable, and surprisingly symbolic. I loved that it stood for help, a universal signal for rescue and support. "Save Our Ship" captured exactly what we were doing: answering the call for families who felt lost at sea, searching for hope. The company's nautical theme came to life in a whole new way. It wasn't just a design choice—it became a message, a mission, and a lifeline.

With a nautical theme in place, I started researching colors. I was interested to find that multiple scientific studies support the idea that the color blue has calming effects. Research suggests that blue can lower blood pressure and heart rate and even reduce feelings of anxiety. Some studies also link blue to increased productivity and improved concentration. It seemed like the perfect color to accompany the *Success on the Spectrum* brand.

I worked so hard designing the logo. I spent hours playing with different nautical icons, tweaking colors, adjusting fonts, and trying to capture the essence of what I was building—a place full of compassion, structure, and second chances. When I finally got it right, I placed it on my newly created website with such pride. That moment was everything. It made it all feel real.

I posted a job ad for a behavior technician online. The first candidate sat in front of me like a stone. Rigid. Cold. Her ideas reeked of punishment procedures and correction through fear. My stomach turned. I thought of my daughter—of her softness, her trust. I couldn't allow someone like that into her world. Into the world I was building.

The second interview felt like a performance—too perfect. Her answers were rehearsed to the point of parody. "Oh, on weekends? I just study ABA. Always. I talk to my friends about how to improve. I live and breathe this work." I watched her eyes as she said it—watched the gleam of practiced deceit. She was telling me what she thought I wanted to hear, not the truth. And in this sacred work with children, I needed truth. I needed honesty more than anything else.

Then came Juliet. Juliet was something else—real, grounded. She spoke with warmth, with balance. Her philosophy mirrored mine: the children must do the work, yes, but they must also play. We must slip the lessons in between laughter and games. We must reward their courage—every small step, every new skill—with a treat, a toy, a hug, a high five, or a radiant smile. Reinforcement, yes—but more than that: *joy.*

She understood, without me having to explain it, that what we were building wasn't a factory or a computer program. It was a place where children could thrive, not in spite of who they were, but because of it. Juliet would be the first staff at SOS. The first of many, I hoped. She carried that rare quality of empathy and structure, of heart and professionalism. She didn't need to be perfect. She just needed to believe in the same things I did, and she did. She was the beginning of something that had once felt impossible, and now, somehow, it was starting to feel real.

She was my first hire, and my gut had chosen her with a clarity I trusted more than any certificate or résumé. After her, I turned my attention to finding a behavior analyst—the kind of person who could build the bones of this thing I was creating.

That's when I interviewed Spencer. She lived in Georgia then, untethered by marriage or children. She talked about moving closer to her aging parents, who lived in Houston. There was a softness to her voice when she spoke of coming back to care for them, and something in me nodded with understanding. Our needs aligned like stars, quietly falling into place.

Everything began to click slowly after that, like a series of locks turning. Now that I had employees, I asked them to meet me for dinner. It was a warm evening, I remember. The kind of dusk that carries possibility in its wind. We sat together in a small steakhouse—full of ambition and nerves. My husband sat beside me while I explained the truth of things. "I don't know everything," I said, stirring the condensation on my glass with a fingertip. "But I'm trusting you. I need your judgment and your experience. I want this to be the kind of place where the protocols aren't just clinical—they're *right*. For my child, for all the children."

Spencer nodded, confident and composed. "I can handle seven, maybe eight children at a time," she said. "Perfect," I replied. "Juliet will be the first technician. But we'll need more. A team."

I turned to Juliet. "Would you help me interview more RBTs? Maybe bring in people you trust?"

She smiled—genuinely. "Of course. Let's build it." It all felt like the beginning of something sacred.

I asked Spencer about which assessment kit she preferred to use, and when she told me, I ordered it immediately. It was huge—bulky, brimming with toys and laminated tasks. I didn't want her lugging it around like a traveling circus, so I bought a large, blue rolling suitcase and packed it neatly with everything she'd need: a mobile assessment kit, neatly zipped.

She conducted assessments on *Success on the Spectrum*'s first two clients—Meez and a 7-year-old boy. She drafted treatment plans and turned to Juliet: "You'll start working with the kids on Monday. You'll spend mornings with the new client at his family home and then drive back to Nichole's to spend afternoons with Meez. We'll keep alternating half days until we find another tech." Juliet agreed, radiant with readiness. I could feel her excitement humming through the air.

That Monday morning, I woke early, as if my body understood the weight of the day before my mind caught up. I texted Juliet: "Everything good? Today's your first day! The first day of the rest of our lives!"

She replied almost instantly: "I'm on my way to the client's house. I'm so excited. Thank you for this opportunity." It felt like spring was blooming in my chest.

Then, I texted Spencer as a gentle nudge of encouragement. "Hey, it's a new day! If Juliet needs anything, she'll text you. I may send you a few of the protocols I wrote in the operations manual—could you look them over?"

Her reply came quickly, but it split something inside me the moment I read it. "Yeah... I decided this wasn't for me. I packed up my car, and I'm on the road. I'm heading back to Georgia." That was it. No warning. No explanation. No apology. Just a cold departure in the middle of our first sunrise. I stared at the screen, numb. My fingers tingled. My face felt hot. She abandoned us.

"You quit?" I wanted to scream. "On the first day? Without notice?" But there was no reply to be had. Just the dull hum of my phone and the heavy knowledge that I had children waiting. Juliet waiting. And no analyst. No one to guide us but me.

I was devastated. Not in the loud, catastrophic way that people imagine devastation to look like—but in the quiet undoing of all the scaffolding I had spent months building. I had done *so* much. I had filed paperwork with trembling hands, answered calls while working my nuclear job, and built all of the clinical contracts around Spencer's credentials. Her license number had unlocked the gates to insurance networks. Her name was the key, and now, without her, everything came to a halt—dead in the water.

You can't run an ABA company without a behavior analyst. That's the rule. That's the bone and breath of it. Without her, my little engine of hope—this beautiful, precarious structure I had built—stood motionless. I sat still for a moment. Then I remembered Kendra. She had been one of the few who impressed me during interviews—intelligent, competent, and independent. She'd declined a full-time role because she already ran her own practice. She only wanted contract work. But I didn't have the luxury of ideals anymore. I needed someone *now*. I called her. "I'm in a bit of a pickle," I said, my voice light with forced levity, masking the tightness in my chest. "Would you be willing to take us on until I can find someone permanent?"

She agreed. And so, Kendra stepped in. She began working with Meez and the other client who enrolled—the one whose case would shift my perception of normal forever.

Chapter 5: Setting Sail

It was an adventure, to say the least—a trial by fire in the truest sense. This boy—he was so much more severe than Meez. There was a darkness that clung to his story, not from him, but from what his family had to live through. His diagnosis came with behaviors so intense they erased any semblance of a normal home.

"Fecal smearing," they called it clinically. It was as if giving it a name somehow made it manageable. He would defecate into his hands and then paint the walls and furniture with it—he seemed to find this act hilarious, soothing, or both. There was no malice. Just a need unmet in ways we didn't fully understand.

When we walked into his home, it felt like stepping into the aftermath of something—like the ghost of what a family space should be. No couch. No dining table. Just four bar stools in the kitchen, a rug rolled across the empty living room floor, and a television on the wall. Nothing else. Emptiness had become a form of protection. He'd destroyed it all, and the family was too tired to replace it anymore.

He also had a strange fixation with breaking glass. The sound of it shattering seemed to give him pleasure—maybe sensory, maybe something deeper, something only he understood. If you turned your back, even for a moment, he would sprint to the kitchen, pull a glass cup from the cabinet, and throw it down just to hear it explode against the tile. And they *still* kept buying glass cups. Why, I never knew.

Perhaps the ritual of being normal was worth the chaos. Or perhaps they were just too worn to change the small things.

Then there was the running. Eloping. But it felt like desperation. If you pushed him too hard—asked him to sit on the potty or do something he didn't like—he would bolt for the front door. He was filled with energy with small and wiry legs that seemed impossibly long for his frame—a little boy who could sprint like a gazelle. You'd blink, and he'd be gone.

Juliet, thank God, was athletic. She was a volleyball coach on weekends, with the legs and lungs of someone who could chase a storm and bring it back. She ran after him— again and again—grabbing him mid-sprint, coaxing him gently back inside. She never complained, just dusted herself off and said, "Oof! He's quick."

There happened to be a day when Juliet got extremely sick and knew she didn't have the energy to keep up with the client. But it was early days, and we didn't have another tech to cover her. Embarrassed, I told Juliet, "We can't stop working. We can't afford it. What can I do to help you get through this day? It's Friday. You've got to make it through one more day, even though you feel sick."

In return, she said, "I threw up all night, and I am dehydrated." So, of course, I drove over to the client's house. I popped open my trunk and opened my medical kit, and I started an IV saline drip in her arm in the client's driveway. I hung the IV bag from the hook in my trunk, and I just let the saline dump into her body.

At the same time, I gave her some prescriptions that I had had from a recent surgery so she wouldn't feel nauseated. And I told her, "Look, you can do this." She instantly agreed and then took care of the client for the rest of the day. She is a soldier.

As time went on, we got more clients and hired more technicians. I didn't want my staff to be driving all over town anymore. We were wasting too much time traveling. The business was growing, so it seemed like renting an office space was the next logical step.

Not to mention, the parents of the high-behaviored boy needed a break. I think that taking their kid out of that home and bringing him to an office setting really gave the parents their sanity back for a few hours a day.

So I shopped around for a place to rent and came across this really cheap property, which was a glass office building. It had multiple stories. They had an office for lease that had been vacant for a while on the fifth floor. I told them what we were doing and that there might be some noise, but they didn't care much. The landlord was desperate for money, so it worked in my favor.

I was so excited to finally have my own little office. I leaned fully into the nautical theme and spent hours picking the perfect shade of blue—comparing hundreds of paint swatches until I found the one that felt just right. I made a detailed list of all the furniture I needed for each room, knowing I had to be strategic with my time since I was still working my other job. So, I planned a one-day, no-nonsense furniture-buying frenzy. I rented a moving truck, mapped out the route, and listed exactly what I needed to buy at each stop to stay within budget.

IKEA was our first destination—affordable and efficient. I had my list ready, so we went directly to the warehouse and hit each aisle like professionals. As we shopped, a man approached me and Meez. "Excuse me, you seem to know how to find things here. I am absolutely lost." I smiled and pushed my carts to the side and walked with him to the kiosk. I showed him how to search for an item and told him that it would spit out which aisle and bin the item was located in. He thanked me and flirted, "My mother always told me that if I ever needed help, I should ask a woman because they know everything." I gave the expected giggle and told him to have a good day. Meez lifted her eyebrows and said a little too loud, "Well, SOMEONE was coddled too much as a child!" I covered her mouth and walked faster toward the checkout.

Then we hit a secondhand furniture store, where I scored a great deal on a reception desk and conference table. We wrapped up at an electronics outlet, grabbing open-box computers and a few clearance TVs. It was a whirlwind, but it was purposeful, and every piece I picked out brought me one step closer to making my dream space a reality.

By the end of the day, the moving truck was packed tight—every inch filled with pieces that I had so carefully envisioned in my head. There was something exhilarating about seeing my vision come together piece by piece. Each item felt symbolic—like I was building the foundation of not just a business but a dream that had lived in my heart for years.

As the sun dipped below the horizon, we pulled up to the building for the first round of unloading. The space echoed with possibility. I could already picture the kids working in the therapy rooms, the team collaborating in the breakroom, and laughter echoing through the playroom.

It was just me, my husband, my brother-in-law, and my sister-in-law unloading the truck. No movers. No crew. Just us sweating and scrambling to turn six empty rooms into something that looked like hope. The scent of fresh paint mixed with sawdust filled the air as we began assembling furniture late into the night. We unboxed toys, arranged little therapy corners, and created makeshift offices. We assembled KALLAX shelves until our hands blistered. My hands were sore, my feet ached, and I was running purely on adrenaline and determination. By Sunday night, we could barely move.

It wasn't glamorous—but it was mine. Every decision and every detail had come from me. I was exhausted, but I was also completely and undeniably alive. This wasn't just a clinic. It was the beginning of something bigger than myself.

One major thing that was missing from the ABA clinic my stepdaughter attended was the ability for parents to observe therapy. In fact, I wasn't even allowed inside the building unless I had a scheduled appointment—and those were nearly impossible to get. I remembered how helpless I felt being shut out of her therapy sessions, wondering what was happening behind closed doors. I didn't want any other parent to feel that way. I wanted my own clinic to be different. I wanted parents to see exactly what we were doing and how we were helping their children grow.

That's when I came up with the idea for the parent viewing room. The parent viewing room became a symbol of everything I believed in: openness, accountability, and the idea that families are partners in the therapy process, not just spectators.

I installed cameras in every therapy room—no easy task, especially when I was completely covered in itchy insulation from lifting ceiling tiles to running the cables. But in the end, it was worth it. I set up the live video feed to display on a large television near the front lobby. When parents dropped off their children, they could relax on the couch and watch real-time footage of their child's therapy sessions. I called it trans**parent**cy. I thought I was hilarious.

On Monday morning, the kids came in—and it was all worth it. I promoted Juliet to office manager because I was still working part-time in nuclear medicine. Two or three days a week, I'd come to the office, sit at the front desk, and watch Juliet work with the kids. But otherwise, she held everything down—answering phones, managing emails, making sure staff clocked in, smoothing the chaos. We were a small but mighty team, and we ran that place with heart.

Over time, the calls started coming in more and more. Parents shared good things, leaving reviews and telling their friends. Our reputation began to spread, and suddenly, we had waitlists. I realized I couldn't do both jobs anymore. So I made the decision—I quit nuclear medicine. I stepped fully into my role as CEO of *Success on the Spectrum*. And Juliet? She remained my office manager, my right-hand "man," and someone I trusted deeply.

We grew fast. We brought in new staff, took in more kids, and, like any business, we had our share of adventures and challenges.

Some hires were terrible. A few staff members treated Juliet badly when I wasn't around—raising their voices and ignoring her instructions. But I backed her completely. If she came to me and said, "They need to go," I fired them. She had earned that kind of trust.

The building gave us headaches, too. One time, Kendra was working with a child in one of the therapy rooms when the door jammed. It was an old building, and the doorframe swelled or shifted or something, and it just stuck. She and the child were trapped for two hours. We called maintenance, but even they couldn't get it open. Eventually, they had to climb in through the ceiling tiles, kick the door in, and replace the entire frame. It was insane, but we laughed it off.

Learning how to submit claims to insurance companies was a nightmare. The process was so convoluted, with endless paperwork and hidden steps. No one walks you through it—there are no classes that teach this kind of stuff. I honestly believe they make it confusing on purpose—to discourage people like me from succeeding. But I learned. Every rejection taught me something. Every obstacle made me more determined.

Chapter 6: Running a Tight Ship

Time moved forward, and I started to see the results of our hard work. Our second client, the boy with the severe behaviors, was finally potty trained. Not only did the fecal smearing stop, but he started using verbal language more. He was finally able to ask for what he wanted instead of acting out. His parents would hug me and sing praises about SOS every day at pick-up time. They were so thankful that their child was making so many improvements. Juliet was most proud of him. But not every family was so grateful.

There is a particular kind of betrayal that blooms slowly, like mold in a sealed room. You don't see it at first—you don't even smell it. And then, one day, everything collapses in on itself, and you're left standing in a ruin you didn't know you built.

I remember verifying that I was in the network with United Optum. The words, "Yes, you are in the network," surrounded me like an incantation in my email inbox and over the phone line. I asked the questions like a woman building a house on shifting sand. "Is this client good to go?" Yes. "What's the copay?" $25 a day. Written. Stamped. Confirmed. I thought I was safe.

And so, I served. *We* served. The child came in day after day, wide-eyed and unaware of the machinery of insurance or the ticking of a financial clock that would never pay out. For nearly three months, we gave this client therapy, guidance, attention, and care. Real care. Not just services but something closer to devotion. I told myself that doing good would be enough.

Then came the flood of letters piled like funeral wreaths. Denied. Not in-network. Not eligible. Not payable. Pages of cold bureaucratic language delivered like slaps. I reached out in a panic. "You said I was in-network. I have it in writing." But they responded with indifference sharpened into cruelty: Too bad, so sad. Pre-authorization is not a guarantee of payment.

$30,000—gone. Just like that, no apology. I knew that the mother couldn't afford to continue therapy as a cash-pay client, so I had to break the news. "I'm so sorry. They lied to us. Your insurance won't pay anything. We have to terminate services. I don't think that it's right to charge you since you didn't know either… so I'm not asking you to pay for any of the services that he's already gotten from us."

The mother didn't say thank you. She didn't marvel at the fact that her child had received months of support for free. She wasn't grateful that I had paid the employees for their time with her child. Instead, she weaponized my mistake. "Oh, you better not—If you charge me a dime," she warned, "I'll sue you." She pulled her child out of the office by his arm. She didn't look back.

That was the first heartbreak that cut deep. A thick, slow ache that throbbed for days. Not because of the money—I could survive a financial loss—but because I had tried, truly tried, and still failed. Because I wanted to help, and helping wasn't enough. There's a particular kind of loneliness that comes from being misunderstood in your most honest moment. That was what I sat with.

The stories didn't end there. We had another client—a boy, though the word doesn't quite fit. Eighteen years old in the body, a man by legal standards. Mentally, though, perhaps eleven. Maybe twelve. His head stretched six feet two inches into the air, towering, heavy-footed, with a presence that filled every room he entered.

He believed he was small, and that was the tragedy of it. He ran, leaped, and toppled onto furniture with the joy of a child unaware of his size. His innocence was colossal, sometimes destructive. His body betrayed him—not by illness, but by scale.

And then there was his unexpected behavior—to be naked. If his mother took him to Target and he didn't want to be there, he wouldn't argue. He wouldn't cry. He would simply undress. And it worked. His mother would gather him in panic and flee the scene, praying he wouldn't be arrested for indecent exposure. The boy had learned that removing his clothes brought swift results. It was not obscene, not lurid, but a genius way to get what he wanted.

He tried that with us, too. We'd ask him to complete a worksheet, and slowly, silently, he'd start peeling his clothes away. Kendra instructed everyone to ignore the behavior, to show him that this wouldn't work. To meet his gaze without flinching. "Let's finish this task," we'd say, eyes fixed on the paper, pretending he wasn't a full-grown naked person in front of us. It was surreal. It was funny. It was human.

And then, another family. Another mother. This time, her fear was urgency made flesh. Her son was an escape artist—quick-footed and silent. At any moment, he could bolt. Through the door. Into the street. Always toward the rushing cars. Her voice trembled when she spoke about it. "He could die," she whispered once, more to herself than to me. "He could just run into traffic, and he could be hit."

That was her greatest fear—his tiny feet flying, darting into the unknown while she stood frozen, breath caught somewhere between her ribs and throat. The street was a living monster with asphalt jaws in her mind. She asked us with a voice knotted in desperation, "How do I get him to stop doing this? How do I make him understand that it's dangerous?"

We answered the way professionals do, calmly, methodically, with a confidence we sometimes had to fake. Kendra wrote a social story for him—gentle, deliberate, filled with stick-figure drawings and phrases like "Hold a grown-up's hand in the parking lot" and "Cars go fast and can hurt you." We read it aloud to him, again and again, repeating it like prayer.

But the mother—sleep-deprived, jittery, brittle from fear—grew impatient. "What if I hit him with my car? Like a lesson," she asked, eyes steady, unblinking. "Just once. Just hard enough so he knows what it feels like. Not hard enough to actually hurt him." Time slowed. Words lost meaning. I stared at her for a moment, wondering if she was serious. "No," I said, and the word fell out of me like a rock dropped in still water. "You *cannot* hit your child with your car." Instead, we offered alternatives—videos, modeling, repetition, patience. I didn't know whether to laugh or to cry. Eventually, Kendra and I talked sense into her.

After reading the social stories, we began to play with dolls, making them wait before crossing the fake street. Once he understood the concept, we started taking him outside to walk around in our building parking lot—usually with multiple adults. We practiced crossing the street, using sidewalks, and pointing out reverse lights in the parking lot. His mother was so relieved to see how well he used his new safety skills.

That wasn't the only moment where the absurd and the terrifying folded into one another. The building itself—the one I had clung to like a raft in the early days—began to rot from the inside. The suite above ours was eventually leased to a probation officer, and with him came his parolees. The building became a rotating door of ghosts: addicts, felons, and prostitutes.

One woman—emaciated and delirious—staggered through the lobby without a thread of clothing on her body. Her skin was the color of paper left in the sun. Her limbs moved like she wasn't inside them. Kendra was the one who saw her first, thank God. I called the landlord with shaking fingers, and they called the police. She was gone within minutes, like a dream dissolving in daylight. But the fear lingered. I didn't want the parents to see this and be afraid to drop off their children.

One of the mothers came to me one morning with her face pale and her eyes wide. "A random man tried to kiss me in the elevator," she whispered, and I felt something in me snap. I was shocked and embarrassed. The place I had tried to build was now polluted with shadows. We had to leave.

When the lease expired, I found a new space half a mile away. Larger, brighter, untouched. It felt like a rebirth. We moved in, unpacked toys and therapy mats like offerings, and filled it with laughter again.

Chapter 7: Barnacles

Meez was now thriving. We made the decision to enroll her in a larger private school. She attended school during the day and worked with Kendra at home in the afternoons. There were, of course, some minor struggles. Autism is not something you can cure, after all. It lingers like a quiet current beneath the calm, occasionally rising with sharp insistence.

One example of Meez's autism symptoms was her difficulty understanding figurative language—everything was taken literally. One afternoon after school, I casually asked how her day had gone. She seemed a little frustrated and said she was upset because the teacher had called on "the shady boy" to answer questions instead of her.

Curious, I asked what the boy had done to be "shady." Meez gave me a puzzled look as if I had three heads. "He didn't do anything," she said earnestly. Confused, I pressed further, "Then why did you call him shady?"

Her answer was pure, literal honesty: "Because of the color of his skin."

I couldn't help but laugh and panic at the same time. "Oh no!" I said quickly, "That's not what shady means! It has nothing to do with race!"

Some days, she'd come home from school wounded—not in body, but in the ego of a child trying to shape herself into the puzzle the world had already cut. A burst of anger here, a misunderstanding there.

But most of it was good. Meez was happy to share that she loved art class. One day, she excitedly told me that the class painted outside. She pulled the stiff papers out of her backpack to show me. The first painting was of her classmates. The second was of Mohammed, Lilo, Meez, and Me holding hands. The third was a painting of a table with fruit in a bowl. As she proudly held them up, she told me, "The paintings are complete with the best things in life: friends, family, and food. I didn't know how to draw a pie, which is unfortunate." I laughed so hard it hurt my sides.

And then came her newfound joy—drama class. Something about the stage unlocked her. She'd never been exposed to it before, never stood in front of a crowd, let alone dared to perform for one. It was as if the theater gave her permission to exist without the constraints of her diagnosis. She loved it. Absolutely loved it.

That December—the first one after she began school— her class put on a Christmas play. She was electric with anticipation; her excitement was a living thing that filled the rooms of our home. She called my mother and begged her to come watch the show. And my mother, who lived four hours away in Louisiana, did what only a grandmother would do— she got in her car and drove over, gifts in hand.

When she arrived, her arms were full of banana nut bread, her own recipe, the same one she makes every Christmas.

There was something holy in that smell—a fragrance of safety and childhood memories.

Surprisingly, Meez's biological mother showed up too—with her newest baby daddy, no less. We sat in the school's little auditorium, the plastic seats hard beneath us. Then the lights dimmed, and Meez stepped up onto the stage next to her classmates. Her hair, which I'd done that morning in two perfect pigtails because she said it made her "feel pretty," bounced as she walked. She was beaming, incandescent. Her voice soared louder than the rest. And at that moment, she wasn't a child with a diagnosis. She wasn't working with her therapy schedules or behavior charts. She was just a little girl, singing her heart out beneath a wash of stage lights, lost in the magic of theater.

After the applause and the school's request for donations that followed, people stood and milled about, exchanging pleasantries. My mother, who has always been supportive of my new family, approached Meez's biological mother. She extended her hand, warm and open. "Hi, my name is Angela. I'm Nichole's mom, the one Meez calls Nana," she said, with that Cajun drawl that I had worked so hard to mask in myself. "I just wanted to tell you that Meez is absolutely adorable. I love her as if she were my own granddaughter, and I would do anything for her." Her words were offered like a benediction, simple and true. "Merry Christmas," she said as she handed her one of the loaves of banana nut bread, wrapped in foil and ribbon.

As my mother extended her hand, soft and gentle, the way only someone with genuine love in her heart could manage, something in Meez's biological mother snapped. Her eyes narrowed, her posture sharpened like a blade, and she recoiled as if my mother's kindness had burned her. "Nana is what *WHITE PEOPLE* call their grandmothers! You are NOT her grandmother!" she shrieked, voice rising over the chatter of post-play parents. "Get this woman away from me! How dare you touch me? Who do you think you are?"

The room stilled. Heads turned. Conversations died on lips. The air, moments before warm with pride and sugar and lights, turned cold—razor-edged and crackling with tension. I stood there, suspended in disbelief, my mouth slightly agape, watching the woman unravel in real time. What the hell was happening? What had my mother done except extend a courteous hand and speak gently, lovingly?

Mohammed, trying to de-escalate, ushered her out of the auditorium. I watched them disappear into the night, the door thudding shut behind them. My mother and I were left amid the aftermath—confused, exposed, small. She turned to me with wide, wounded eyes. "What did I do wrong?"

"Nothing," I said quickly, reaching for her hand. "You didn't do anything wrong."

It didn't make sense. We had just recently managed to get Meez's biological mother to agree to let us take her to Disney World—her first time, her dream. And now, in the parking lot, she was spiraling. Her voice, even through the walls, was unmistakable—accusatory and venomous.

"You messed up!" she screamed at Mohammed. "She's not going to Disney with you anymore. You tell her why. You tell her the trip is canceled. You knew better than to bring *that woman* here!"

That woman—as if my mother's love was an offense—as if decency could be criminal.

When Mohammed returned, his face was red and tight with frustration. But it wasn't just that—there was something else behind his eyes, something that was too quick to give a name, or it was rage, maybe. Humiliation. Confusion laced with overstimulation. A cocktail of emotions I didn't have the time to dissect before he turned to my mother and erupted.

"Why did you introduce yourself without asking my permission?" he snapped, his voice sharp and fast, like a door slamming over and over again. I moved between them instinctively, placing my hand gently but firmly against his chest. "She doesn't need your permission. And she didn't do anything wrong."

He pivoted to me then, his frustration shifting like a spotlight. "This is your fault. Why didn't you control your mother? Look what you've done. Now the Disney trip is ruined."

His words struck like stones, fast and unrelenting. I could hardly breathe under the weight of their absurdity. "How is this our fault?" I asked, my voice low, stunned. "We didn't make her act like that. We couldn't have predicted it. We didn't even do anything."

But he wasn't listening. He'd already retreated into himself. "We'll have to agree to disagree," he muttered coldly, retreating into the car, slamming the door between us, and whatever conversation still lingered in the air. He didn't speak to me for the rest of the night.

And that silence—that punishing, bewildering silence—was worse than any scream. It was the first time I looked at him and truly thought, *Who is this man?* The logic I once trusted in him had crumbled, leaving only raw, disjointed emotion. There was no reason for his reaction. No fairness. Just blame hurled like a grenade.

It was the first time I felt the edge of something I hadn't seen before in him: a temper that didn't make sense, rooted not in justice but in control. An emotional impulse that overruled logic, compassion, and love, and it left me quietly, terrifyingly unsettled.

So I let it go. I told myself he was overwhelmed that day, maybe even triggered, and that we'd talk about it later—once the adrenaline faded and his reason returned. But the conversation never changed. Even months later, he would still refer to the incident as my mother's fault.

Time went by, as it always does. Mohammad and I settled into a comfortable rhythm. He dropped Meez off at school each morning before heading to the office. I had more flexibility in my schedule, so I left SOS early in the afternoons to pick her up.

Evenings were quiet and predictable—he sat with his laptop typing up medical notes for his clinic while I sat beside him submitting insurance claims for my clinic. We didn't talk much during those hours, but to me, the silence felt like a partnership. I felt as though we were building something side by side.

One weekend, we were invited to a dinner party hosted by a physician couple that Mohammad knew. I was excited for a night out—eager to break the monotony and a reason to dress up and feel glamorous for a change. Mohammad, predictably, needed convincing. Social events weren't his thing. But we went, and as we drove up to the house, I was stunned. A grand Mediterranean-style mansion stood behind a wrought-iron gate and lush gardens, complete with a bubbling fountain and a circular motor court. Waitstaff bustled in and out, and soft jazz drifted through the evening air. It felt like we had stepped into a movie scene.

We exchanged a glance—equal parts impressed and curious. We both made decent money but could never afford a house like this. We joked that Mohammed should start offering private services to the mafia, too.

Inside, we found ourselves among people dressed to perfection—floor-length gowns, tailored suits, and delicate clinks of champagne glasses. I didn't know a soul. Mohammad only knew the hosts. For a while, we stood off to the side, talking quietly to each other like outsiders at a country club.

Eventually, a woman approached us. She was dripping in diamond jewelry that I guessed cost more than my Range Rover. Her husband trailed behind her in a designer tux. She introduced herself warmly, her voice polished. When Mohammad introduced himself as Dr. Daher—a quadruple-boarded physician with a private practice—her interest piqued immediately. Then she turned to me. I told her I was not a doctor, but I owned a behavioral health practice.

She blinked, confused. "That's not possible." she laughed condescendingly. "You can't own a medical practice without being a practitioner."

I explained that I owned the business and simply hired the medical professionals. She looked at me as if I were speaking Greek. "Wait, so… what do you do exactly?"

I could feel Mohammad shift beside me, uncomfortable. I looked at him and saw the tension in his body. I softened my tone and quickly offered, "Oh, I'm just here as his plus one. I'm his wife." I added a fake laugh.

She smiled, satisfied with that answer, and turned her back to me to resume conversation with Mohammad and the other doctors. I had been blatantly dismissed. I stared daggers into her back. The sting of it lingered. What hit harder was the realization that Mohammad thrived on recognition. He needed his credentials to speak louder than anything else in the room. Beneath his overconfident facade, he was insecure.

That night, as we drove home in silence, I stared out the window and replayed the conversation over and over. I wasn't hurt, not exactly. I was... aware. Aware of how uncomfortable he had been when I presented myself as an equal. It dawned on me that my success might make him feel threatened. And I began to wonder: how often would I have to pretend to be less than I am? I loved him and would do anything to protect my marriage... but how long could I keep up the pretenses?

That night marked a quiet shift. I didn't say anything to Mohammad. I smiled, kissed him goodnight, and crawled into bed beside him. I made a mental note to keep a low profile to protect his ego. I wanted to keep him happy and make him feel secure.

Chapter 8: The Birth of SOS Franchising

A few years went by, and the clinic grew faster than I expected. I was able to pay back the loan that Mohammed had given me quickly.

More calls. More parents. More desperation. Voices trembling over the phone, asking, *can you help my child?* And I finally had to say the thing I never wanted to say: "We're full. I'm sorry. We have a waitlist." It gutted me every time because I had *been* that mother. I had *been* on the other end of the line, begging for a lifeline, and now I was the one holding it just out of reach.

So, in 2018, I opened a second clinic—this time on the far side of the city. It was bigger, better, bursting with possibility. I got another moving truck and filled it with furniture and supplies, but this time, I didn't ask Mohammed to help. I didn't want to make it a big deal. In fact, I don't recall him ever visiting this location at all. I had plenty of employees to help me this time.

Juliet and I bounced around each other, alternating between clinics and making sure everything was taken care of. It was a crazy whirlwind of hiring more technicians, fixing broken things, doing supply runs to Costco, and creating new protocols as unexpected scenarios arose.

 Within nine months, the second location became full, too. The truth landed hard and cold: the need was greater than I could handle. I could have opened a third, fourth, or fifth clinic. I could have filled my calendar with so many tasks that there'd be no space left for breath. No space left to care for Meez. I knew if I added more clinics, I would vanish from my daughter's life like a phantom—a mother building the world for everyone else's children while mine waited alone, and that, in the quietest parts of me, felt like a betrayal. After all, I had started all of this for her.

That's when I knew—I needed more Nicholes. I needed more people to open clinics. The only way to scale what I'd built—to breathe life into it beyond my reach—was to franchise the business. It scared me that no one had done it before, not in this field. Did they know something that I didn't? I was either a genius or an idiot for doing this… and I wasn't sure which.

The idea felt absurd and electric. I had previously learned that franchising a business costs hundreds of thousands of dollars. Lawyers had to draw up documents and compliance agreements, file trademarks, and get licenses to sell—it was a playground for corporate sharks and men in pressed suits. And I was not one of them.

I am a penny pincher by nature. I was not born to wealth. Every dollar has always been a soldier in a war I couldn't afford to lose. I was still reaching for scraps of wisdom wherever I could find it. My husband had a friend who was a business lawyer. I thought maybe I could ask for free advice under the warm cover of dinner and friendship.

So I prepared. I worked for weeks, polishing every corner of my business plan. I made graphs and charts, bound them with pride, had them printed at Kinko's, and placed them inside a navy blue folder that felt like armor. My beautiful logo shone on the cover like a seal of hope.

He arrived at our home with the ease of a man who had never needed to hustle. "I started a business," I said, my voice soft but filled with intention. "It's going really well, and I want to franchise it."

"Oh yeah, yeah," he interrupted, waving my words away like smoke. "Your husband told me. You quit your job and started your own little thing. That's so great." *Little thing.* The words curled inside me like cold fingers.

"No," I said, gently correcting him. "It's not just a little thing anymore. It grew quickly, and now I have two offices. I wanted to show you the business plan and ask you to look it over. See if I've missed anything. Maybe you could help me make a Franchise Agreement…"

But he wasn't listening. Not really. His eyes glazed over somewhere during my first sentence, and he began playing with his phone. He wasn't interested in my graphs. He didn't ask about the children or the mothers or the fire behind the plan. He saw a young girl with a hobby. A doctor's bored housewife with a project.

I forced my business plan into his hands between his sips of wine. He glanced at it like it was a novelty—something to chuckle at. The polite, dismissive laugh was heard in the room, and for a moment, I felt the full weight of it. "Wow. This business idea looks nice!" he said, his voice laced with that condescending humor. He laughed as though he had just uncovered some quaint, harmless idea that had no real substance behind it.

I sat there, watching the dismissive smirk spread across his face. It wasn't just his words; it was his entire demeanor. He didn't see me, not really. He didn't hear anything I had explained earlier, didn't process that I was already running this business—*a real business*—with real clients, real outcomes.

"I've already said this," I repeated, my voice more stern than it should have been. I was tired of being underestimated, and a storm inside of me was beginning to rise. "This business is open and running already. These are the actual numbers. These are real clients. This is the business I've built, and I am actively trying to franchise it."

He didn't get it. Or maybe, more truthfully, he didn't *want* to get it. He shrugged and mumbled something about how difficult the process of franchising is and how many people it would take to run it—but I knew exactly what he was doing. He wasn't looking at me. He wasn't listening to my plan. He was looking past me. He was calculating how he could slide out of the conversation so that he could talk to my husband instead.

I could feel the subtle weight of his disregard. And it burned. Not because of him, not because of his shallow, arrogant underestimation of me—but because it wasn't the first time. It wouldn't be the last time. I had been underestimated by people like him my entire life, and each time, it gnawed at something deep in me.

I stared into the back of his head, angry and quiet. My thoughts went cold, precise. This was the moment I set my heels in. I was going to prove him—and everyone else— wrong. Do you think I can't do this? Watch me.

After more Google queries, I found a man online—once a lawyer, now disbarred, his past folded away in some courtroom shadow. He wasn't allowed to charge the full rate of a lawyer since he was not licensed, but he still had all the right knowledge. I—ever resourceful, ever frugal—saw the opportunity for a discount. He helped me draft my franchise agreement for $40,000, a sum that felt both enormous and miraculous. We spent months planning how we wanted the franchise to work and writing up the legal contracts. When it was done, I brought it to a real lawyer for review.

Trademark attorneys? Also expensive. So, I Googled DIY instructions and watched hours of YouTube videos, studying them like sermons. I taught myself how to file for a trademark patent. And somehow, miraculously, it worked. My trademark was approved. I remember staring at the confirmation email like it was a birth certificate. Apparently, I was good at this.

As expected, I didn't want to pour money into a fancy website for the franchising company. That wasn't my way. So I opened a free WordPress web designer and began to fumble my way through fonts and pixels, like a child sewing patches onto a worn doll. I uploaded a photo, deleted it, changed the tagline, then changed it again. I eventually came up with a design and content that pleased me and released it into the world.

Now that the franchise agreement was finalized, I set about the next task—building a framework and a roadmap that others could follow. It wasn't enough just to do it. Now, I had to make sure that when others opened their own SOS location, it would flourish with the same integrity and the same care that I had poured into every step.

It wasn't going to be easy. Nothing about this journey ever had been. I turned to Kendra and showed her the plans to franchise, the steps, and the methods I had outlined. I pleaded with her to come on full-time, and after weeks of uncertainty, she finally agreed. She didn't have to. But she did because she believed in what we were building. She believed that our model could have a huge impact.

With Kendra and Juliet fully on board (nautical pun intended), we were ready to start crafting the training materials and operations manual—the protocols, the methodologies, and the way we handled every scenario. I created the materials for the CEOs. I wrote down everything I'd learned through mistakes and triumphs alike. How to get health insurance contracts, how to admit clients, how to submit claims. I created this collection of knowledge so franchisees wouldn't trip over the same obstacles I had.

Juliet created training materials for the technicians—imparting all the knowledge she had gleaned over years of hard work and dedication. Kendra built out all of the clinical protocols. Together, we were building this system, this network, so that this business could thrive and last beyond us. And slowly, piece by piece, the franchise began to take shape.

One of my original employees, a behavior technician who had been with us from the very beginning, pulled me aside one day after a shift. She had worked with other ABA companies, she told me, and none of them did it right. None of them treated the kids the way we did. They didn't respect the families. They didn't set up the rooms the way we did, with care, with love, with purpose.

And I stood there, listening to her, and a sense of satisfaction filled me. This was it. This was what I had wanted. Not just a business. Not just a paycheck. But a place where people mattered. Where the children, the families, and everyone involved felt seen.

I remember the way her words settled in me like warm tea on a cold morning. Quiet validation. In a world where I had stitched every piece of this dream together with trembling fingers and sleepless nights, her words were safe. And then, without hesitation, she said, "I love the brand you've built. I want to be your first franchisee."

The air stilled. I named a price that felt fair, not greedy, not timid. Just enough. I handed her the business plan I had written from scratch, the same one I had stayed up countless nights editing, rewriting, and willing into life.

She eventually signed the franchise agreement. I helped her form an LLC, hire people, get in-network, and shop for office space. Finally, in the quiet sprawl of Richmond, Texas (just outside Houston), the first franchise of *Success on the Spectrum* was born.

She was sharp, full of fire and promise. Clients flocked to her. The waiting list grew. I watched from afar, like a mother peering through a window, nervous but proud. When she faltered—when the training I offered lacked clarity—I created more materials. Not just for her but for the next in line too, whomever they might be. Someone was always just down the road.

SOS Franchising was alive and well. I got a few other franchisees in the Houston metro area. We were like a huge family (some of the CEOs were autism moms, like me), helping each other figure things out and meeting for lunch to vent and laugh about all the crazy things that happen.

Chapter 9: Weathering The Storm

Time, again, carried us forward. Meez blossomed. Her love for drama didn't just persist—it flourished. By the time she reached junior high, her school had announced the big annual production, a collaboration with the Juilliard program, no less. Shrek: The Broadway Musical. It felt impossibly grand for a private school in a modest neighborhood, but somehow, it was happening. Meez auditioned and was cast as a fairy tale character.

I threw myself into the experience. I volunteered as a backstage mom, and it was like finding a part of myself I didn't know was missing. I thrived in that world—doing hair, applying makeup with steady focus, and helping with costume changes under the dim, buzzing glow of backstage lights. I ate lunch with the other moms, laughed over coffee cups and tangled wigs, and somewhere in all that behind-the-scenes chaos, Meez and I found a new rhythm together.

My mother drove in again to see the play. After rehearsing her lines with me every night, Meez was a pro on the stage. She was glowing with delight. Her smile could not have stretched any bigger. I stood on the side of the audience with my camera, recording her big moment. She was the cutest fairy tale character ever.

Everything was going so well… Then the pandemic struck.

COVID swept in like a cold fog, erasing everything in its path. I had just signed contracts with all of these franchisees. They had just taken out huge loans. I couldn't sleep. The weight of it pressed on my chest at night—what if I had led them into financial ruin? I had a doctor husband, a financial net. If I failed, I'd be bruised but not broken. They had gambled everything on my dream. I paced the house at night, my thoughts loud and cruel.

Guilt became my companion. Every phone call tightened something inside me. Every silence from them made me think the worst. And I told my team, "No more selling franchises. Shut down the website. I don't want to sell another dream I might not be able to keep alive."

The fear was so real I could taste it, metallic and bitter. And still, under it all, a quiet resolve stirred like a heartbeat. I had built this. I could carry it. Somehow. To tell you the truth, when I made the decision to pause any new franchise agreements, I didn't know if I was making the right call. The weight of those decisions was immense. But in the end, it was the right choice. We had to ensure that the business model was truly sustainable and that it could weather any storm before we expanded further.

Meez's school shut its doors. Zoom replaced classrooms, and the structure gave way to screens. Meez struggled immediately. Without the unspoken accountability of eye contact and raised hands—her motivation dissolved. The spark she had in the classroom, the one that lit her drive to do well, was snuffed out by the cold blue glare of a

Chromebook. She'd sit down with the best intentions and end up spiraling into hours of YouTube videos, her assignments untouched. She'd say, "I got distracted." And I'd nod, trying not to let my concern settle too heavily between us. We were all fraying in our own ways.

The clinics were still doing well on paper. But I woke up every day with dread lodged beneath my ribs, afraid the world's unraveling would reach our doors next. I held everything together with the sheer force of will—therapy teams, schedules, clients, my daughter's sense of routine— and it showed. I was tired. She was tired. We both needed a break we weren't going to get.

Then April came, and with it, taxes. It was always my job. I'd sort through the documents, speak to the CPA, file everything, and Mohammed would skim, sign, and walk away. But this year—this year was different. When the numbers came in, and I handed him the final 2019 return, his eyes scanned the page and then froze. His jaw went slack, his silence louder than any scream. He looked at me, and I saw it in his eyes before he said a word: shock, confusion... disappointment. "You made almost four hundred thousand dollars last year?" he asked with words that were slow, almost slurred with disbelief.

"Yes," I said simply, trying to sound modest, casual, normal. "Isn't that great?" I smiled—small, careful. Hoping. *Please be proud of me.* But his silence stretched. Something in him had shifted.

He was a doctor. And not just any doctor—an Arab man whose sense of self had been built on intellect, prestige, and pride. He was twelve years older than me, and in his eyes, I had always been the younger wife, the student, the subordinate. My success—*my* success—had pulled the rug from beneath his certainty. He wasn't the biggest wallet in the room anymore. And I had done it quietly, without fanfare, without asking "permission."

I hoped he would celebrate me, but he didn't— he couldn't. He wasn't proud of me. Not even a little. And from that moment— quiet, exact, like the instant before a thunderclap— the light inside him seemed to flicker and die. Something elemental shifted.

He grew cold. It was subtle at first, the way winter sneaks into your bones before you realize you've stopped feeling your fingers. He began coming home later, and later, his excuses were vague and pre-wrapped in irritation. "I already ate," he'd say, brushing past me. "I grabbed something while I was out." No kiss on the cheek. No shared meal. No trace of warmth. Just me, alone, eating leftovers in the kitchen under too-bright lights that made everything feel even emptier.

If I asked—gently, carefully, walking on invisible glass—"Why are you working so late?" he'd bristle instantly. "It's my job. It's important. I'm saving lives. You think I enjoy this? You want to blame me for working hard?" And so I stopped asking.

The tension settled into the walls of the house, whispering at night, coiling around the doorknobs. The man I had married—the man who used to show affection—was no longer beside me. I wasn't his partner anymore. I was a mirror he didn't want to look into. I was the rival who made more, who succeeded louder, and his pride couldn't stomach it.

Chapter 10: Fair Winds

To my pleasant surprise, SOS survived COVID with flying colors, not just because we were considered an essential healthcare service but because I had an incredible team. Most of the employees stuck with me through the most challenging months.

I wanted to show my employees and clients that I was doing everything possible to keep them safe. I contacted a local stand-alone ER that was advertising that they were the first ones offering vaccines to the public. I coordinated a drive-through event with them. Nurses stood in a line in the SOS parking lot, syringes and alcohol pads in hand. They swabbed noses, ran tests, and administered the vaccines through everyone's car window.

Parents were so appreciative. I filmed everything with my phone and posted it on Facebook. Mohammed was a doctor and, therefore, had gotten vaccinated before it was available to the public. I sat Meez down and had a grown-up conversation with her. "COVID is not affecting children as much as adults. There is no guarantee that this vaccine will prevent you from getting anything. You are old enough now to make certain decisions about your own body. Do you want to get the vaccine or not?" She looked pensive for a moment, then said, "Well… it's not like it can give me autism… So let's do it." She laughed at her own joke, and I did, too. I held her hand while they cleaned her arm and injected the vaccine. She sat perfectly still and said that it didn't hurt at all. I was proud of her.

The schools were closed, and parents who had kids on the spectrum were also struggling, like Meez. They reached out to us to enroll their kids in the clinic. Some of our existing clients had neurotypical siblings with nowhere to go, and parents asked if they could pay us cash to keep them during the day, too.

So, we found a solution. We started taking in all the kids— both autistic and neurotypical— and created a safe space for them. We made separate classrooms and created small groups. I hired teacher's assistants to keep the neurotypical kids on task with virtual school. I hired a few people whose sole job was to sanitize everything all day. It was a creative solution, born out of necessity, but it worked.

The school system eventually caught wind of what we were doing, and we were contracted as a remote school site. They funded us to help kids who were displaced from school, continuing to offer them the services they needed. More and more kids were sent our way, and we set up small groups, with one technician per room, to ensure they had the support they needed.

I discovered that our business model was very secure. The fact that we were a healthcare service meant that insurance covered the cost for many families. Even as parents lost their jobs due to the pandemic, their children could continue ABA therapy without added financial burden. We were able to stay open and continue supporting our families while so many other businesses were shutting down. It felt like a miracle, and I couldn't believe how things were unfolding.

That time was both a challenge and an unexpected blessing. We had found a stability I didn't anticipate, and in some ways, it was like an accident—a happy one. We proved that the model worked, and the business was strong enough to survive even the toughest of times.

As COVID finally wound down, I knew we were in a different place. Our foundation had been tested, and we had passed with flying colors. It was time to think about the future again—about scaling the franchise, about expanding—but now, we had the confidence to move forward, knowing that we had built something that could last, something that could truly help people, no matter what came next.

The franchise model that I had been so hesitant to expand was now a hope for others. We had survived—no, we had thrived—and we had done so because we adapted because we stayed true to our mission. And, perhaps most importantly, because we never lost sight of the families who needed us.

That summer, I received an unexpected phone call from a man in Florida, the sunlight practically audible in his voice. He wasn't calling to open a franchise. He was a dad searching for treatment for his autistic son. "I found your website," he said, "Did you know that you're the only ABA franchise in the whole country? And I know you're far away, but this is a genius business model, and I want to be a part of it!"

He had experience in franchise sales—he was currently working in franchise sales for an indoor skydiving franchise, a company called iFly. He said, "I know this is going to be huge. I want to work for you. I want to be your sales director."

I laughed, nervous and uncertain. "Sir, we don't have a sales director. It's just me holding this all together with duct tape and prayer. Besides, I don't know you, and you're all the way in Florida."

But he was persistent. "Sales doesn't have to be in person. I can do it all virtually. I'll even take a pay cut. Just give me a small base and commission for everything I sell. I want to be part of this."

There was something in his voice—something familiar. The fatigue of an autism parent with the desperate hope that the world could be different. I recognized it like a mirror. I couldn't afford him, not really. But I knew he had knowledge I didn't. And we were after the same thing: something better for our children. So I said yes.

The franchising business had finally begun to take shape, and all of the right people surrounded me to create the perfect team. It was not without its growing pains, of course, but its machinery—built from my vision and fueled by everyone's hard work—had started to pay off.

Chapter 11: Reaching the 8-Year Limit

People say marriage is hard—and they're right. But no one tells you that the hardest parts don't always come with screaming fights or slamming doors. Sometimes, the deepest pain comes in silence. It comes in the weeks when the man you love becomes a stranger, when you feel the space in the bed grow wider even though you're lying inches apart. That was the seventh year of my marriage. The infamous slump. The season where love felt like a memory, we were both trying to remember.

Mohammed had been emotionally distant for months. I chalked it up to stress, work, life. But my instincts were louder than my excuses. Something felt wrong, though I had no proof. Just a heavy, sinking feeling that I wasn't crazy... even if I wanted to be.

The truth didn't come in an affair confession. It came in a cold, sterile doctor's office. I had gone in for my routine annual check-up—something I had done countless times before without a second thought. When my gynecologist called to tell me I had tested positive for HPV, my stomach twisted into a knot so tight I could barely breathe. I had never tested positive before. This was new. And that meant... it had been a recent exposure. Sometime recently, my husband had shared himself with someone else, and I was now carrying the physical proof of it.

I felt dirty. Humiliated. *Violated* in a way I couldn't even explain. I remember staring at myself in the mirror, wondering how I had gotten here. Wondering how a woman like me—strong, smart, accomplished—ended up feeling this small. It was a shame I didn't deserve.

When I told Mohammed about the results, he looked genuinely shocked—mouth slightly open, eyes darting as if searching for the right expression. And then came the denial. Firm. Absolute. "I haven't been with anyone else," he said, as if that should close the case.

He followed it up with a thin medical explanation—one of those carefully crafted, emotionally manipulative ones that sounded just sad enough to seem plausible. He claimed his previous wife had been diagnosed with HPV. Maybe, he suggested, it had been transmitted from her and it had been dormant in my body all these years and only now decided to show itself. He looked down as he said it as if weighed by guilt—not the guilt of hurting me, but the guilt of being caught in a pattern he didn't want to face.

Dormant for nearly eight years? I knew it wasn't the truth. I saw it for what it was: a man too scared to face the mirror. And yet, even with that knowledge, I chose to stay. Not because I believed him but because I wasn't ready to let go. Because I still believed in the man he used to be. Because I still thought that if I loved him hard enough, we could fix what was broken. I believed in the possibility that we could find our way back to each other. I didn't realize then that I was the only one reaching.

At home, Meez still struggled. A teen now, her sass made me lose my temper more than once. Mohammed continued to be antagonistic, and we operated in survival mode for months. The COVID lockdown was finally lifted, so I thought maybe we just needed to reset. Perhaps a change of scenery could untie whatever knots were choking us. A trip.

I spoke to my friend, Taylor. Her boyfriend, oddly enough, was the only person my husband vaguely considered a friend—though their conversations were always mediated by us. The men never called each other directly, never confided, never laughed the way real friends did. But still, it was something. A point of familiarity.

"Let's all go," I said. "Somewhere warm. Somewhere beautiful." We agreed on Puerto Vallarta, Mexico—a place painted in greens and ocean blues, with a resort that promised indulgence and the kind of ease we hadn't felt in years.

We planned excursions. Meez was ecstatic—her eyes lit up when I told her we'd be zip-lining across mountaintops and waterfalls and that we would all ride donkeys up a narrow, winding trail. She was always a little thrill-seeker, chasing adrenaline the way other girls chased glitter. Her energy was magnetic, and I wanted this for her. I wanted this for *us*. A memory wrapped in sunlight, far from the cold silence of home.

Mohammed feared heights. I knew this. So I asked him, repeatedly, "Are you sure you want to do the zip lining? You

really don't have to." But he insisted, again and again—
"Yes, of course. I'll do it. Don't worry."

When we finally arrived at the resort, everything
shimmered with possibility. The ocean was a deep velvet
blue; the air smelled of salt and citrus. That first evening, we
went to one of the resort's finer restaurants. Meez wore a
little sundress, and I curled her hair into soft waves. Upon
arrival, the host told Mohammed that he couldn't enter with
flip-flops. He was embarrassed and quickly went to the room
to change shoes. I had no idea it was the first spark before an
explosion.

Dinner was elegant but relaxed—one of those all-
inclusive affairs where the waiters encouraged you to order
freely and try everything. So we did. Small plates arrived in
waves, colors and aromas dancing between us. And for a
while, it was lovely. We laughed. We talked. We let the food
and the music soften the edges of everything we had been
carrying.

Taylor and I have a very close relationship. We both like
to drink iced tea, but I don't like lemon, and she likes extra
lemon. So, whenever we're eating at a restaurant together,
we'll just order our iced tea, and I'll put my lemon on her
drink. She knows that I don't like mushrooms. So she'll
immediately take the mushrooms off of my plate and put
them onto hers. We were very comfortable around each
other. It was never anything that I thought to worry about,
but that day, as we were all eating, Taylor made a passing

comment about Mohammed eating his beets dipped in mayonnaise. "That's a bit weird. Is it good?"

He snapped like a brittle twig. The entire restaurant froze when he erupted, yelling at her as if she had personally insulted his ancestors. It was like a bomb had gone off, and we were all choking on the dust and debris. I was sitting there with my heart pounding in my throat, watching everything unravel faster than I could catch it.

I could see it in Taylor's face—the way her eyes went wide, and her whole body recoiled, that old panic rising up from somewhere too deep to hide. I knew she had survived abuse in her childhood that no one should ever have to, and he had just taken her right back there. I was mortified. Embarrassed. Furious. I squeezed his hand under the table, silently begging him to stop, but he just pulled away and kept going. Taylor and her boyfriend sat quietly until he finished yelling. Taylor quietly apologized and left the restaurant.

Then, like a horrible ripple effect, it followed us back to the hotel room. I tried—God, I tried—to reason with him, to explain how unnecessary and cruel that outburst was, how it could've been handled privately and gently. But there was no reaching him. His voice rose. His tone sharpened. And the very moment it became about me, "You should've known better. You always let her do whatever she wants. You don't respect me." I felt the familiar ache crawl up my spine. The one that whispers, *this isn't right.*

Meez, also overstimulated by the yelling, had been holding it together like a dam about to burst. She'd seen too much, heard too much, felt too much. When I gently asked her to brush her teeth and get ready for bed—just a normal, end-of-the-night routine—it was like a switch flipped.

She exploded. Screaming. Full-body, high-pitched, guttural screams. Not words. Not cries. Just raw, unfiltered emotion pouring out of her. It was like watching a spirit trying to claw its way out of her throat. My baby—bigger than me now, towering over me, wild-eyed and completely out of control. And I froze because I didn't know whether to hold her or hide.

And Mohammed? Instead of helping, instead of calming her or me, he turned to me with that same cold fury. "This is your fault," he spat. "You're always telling her what to do. She's triggered because of *you.*"

Her tantrum lasted an hour. We were terrified the neighbors would call the police, thinking that a woman was being murdered. Mohammed made a comment about us going to a Mexican jail and losing custody. His thoughts spiraled out loud.

She eventually screamed herself to sleep. And in that room, with the walls closing in and all three of us facing our true selves at once, I realized something: This wasn't just about food. Or travel. Or taxes. This was about control, about power, about whose voice got to matter, and mine was being silenced, even in front of my child.

The next day, Mohammed refused to go ziplining, which was expected. I half thought that he started the fight the night before to use it as a valid excuse not to go. It would excuse him from the activity without threatening his image as a strong man.

However, he also refused to let me take Meez. He said I was the reason she acted out, and he needed to ensure that she was calm that day. I tried to shake it off. Taylor, her boyfriend, and I went on the excursion without them. I feel guilty to say it, but those few hours without him were incredible. The donkeys brought us up the mountain, and we ziplined to the next lowest peak and then another zipline to the next. We glided over the lush jungle. The waterfalls were larger than the pictures. There was a surprise giant water slide at the end of the trail. We all had a blast.

Trip over, we flew back home and unpacked our bags. I offered to order pizza, our weekly ritual since it was my favorite food, but Mohammed refused. In fact, he never ate pizza again. I'm certain that it was just a vindictive way to make me miserable. A quiet cruelty that he used to chip away all of my joy.

He also never came to bed again. The next morning, I found him asleep on the sofa. When I asked if he was upset with me, he said no, that he had just worked late on his laptop and "accidentally" passed out. Suspiciously, it happened every single night after that. I knew that it was intentional. He wanted to deny me physical touch and all the things that I loved most. He was so calculated. So cold.

In the fall, schools opened back up. I remember when Meez's school planned a field trip to Washington, D.C.

Parents had to go to a meeting about TSA procedures, chaperones, and itineraries. Mohammed was working, as usual. I always went to these things. I pulled a teacher aside. Explained how Meez needed help going through TSA. She'd had a meltdown in an airport before. Autism isn't visible, and with her Arab last name, TSA made me nervous. I just wanted to make sure she was safe.

And so the teacher said, "No problem. I'll find a chaperone who can stick with her through the TSA checkpoints and make sure she's comfortable. Let me get back to you." It felt like such a small ask, you know? A simple solution for a child who needs a little more support.

Later, the teacher followed up with an email to both Mohammed and me, saying they had found someone willing to help Meez at the airport. I thought—great, problem solved. But when Mohammed saw the email, he got furious.

"Why would you tell them that?" he snapped. "What gives you the right to always take over?" I was genuinely confused. I quietly responded, "Because she needs help. What's the issue?"

"You may be the boss at SOS, but you don't get to tell me and my child what to do," he snapped. He didn't talk to me at all after that. Instead, he replied directly to the school: *Nichole is no longer able to attend meetings or interact with Meez's teachers. She's just a stepmother and has no decision-making ability for my child.*

That... that was the moment I knew. He was done with me.

He wasn't just pulling away emotionally anymore—he was beginning to dismantle my place in Meez's life. And it killed me. She wasn't just *his* child anymore. She was *our* child. I had been the one there, every day, showing up for her. Loving her. Advocating for her. And now I was being erased.

Looking back, I realize it was all psychological warfare. He'd cheated on his first wife and didn't want to marry the second. His family teased him for being on his third marriage. I think he wanted out—But he didn't want to be the bad guy again. He wanted *me* to be the reason for this divorce. He was trying to make me leave.

But I wouldn't let that happen. I believe marriage is forever, for better or worse. The more he pushed me away, the harder I tried. I kept thinking—if I'm just extra careful, extra loving, extra agreeable, maybe we can get through this. I tiptoed around his moods, never knowing what would set him off. If I had a bad day, I kept it to myself. But if *he* had a bad day, I turned him into his personal cheerleader. "Oh my God, I can't believe that happened to you," I'd say, nodding, sympathizing, making space for his frustration.

But no matter what I did, it was wrong. If Meez didn't do her homework, he'd come home furious and yell at me— *You're a bad mother. You should be keeping her on track.* But if I set timers and gently redirected her, "Okay, ten minutes of YouTube and then back to work"—and she melted down when he walked in the door, he'd yell at me for that, too. "You're too strict. You're a slave driver. You're making things worse."

There was name-calling. Gaslighting. Constant contradictions. If I did nothing, I was lazy. If I did something, I was overbearing. If the house wasn't clean, I was a hypocrite. If I cleaned, he would accuse me of losing his things. If I asked for something to change, I was unpleasable. I was damned if I did, damned if I didn't.

I knew, deep down, that he wanted me to initiate a breakup. He was using mental and emotional manipulation in the most intimate of spaces. And still—I didn't want him to win. I didn't want to let him throw our marriage away. So I smiled through it. Let it roll off me. Pretended it didn't sting, but it did. God, it did.

One day, out of nowhere, Mohammed insisted that my Range Rover was on the verge of collapse, despite there being no signs of trouble. He wouldn't listen to reason, brushing off my protests like they were nothing, and without my consent, he traded it in for a Kia Sorento. It felt cruel and deliberate, as if he took some twisted pleasure in stripping away the things I loved. But the joke was on him. That Sorento turned out to be one of the best cars I ever owned— more trunk space, better features, and a smoother ride, all for half the price. What he meant as punishment became a gift. I think it made him angry that I loved it so much. I overheard him complaining to his brother about it.

Mohammed's lawyer friend asked us to dinner again. He had this "amazing business opportunity" and wanted Mohammed to invest. Mohammed was very interested in this new business venture, as he was unhappy with medicine (and everything, frankly) and wanted new ways to make passive income. The cost of the shares was outrageous, but because they needed a medical director to license the business, so Mohammed would get a discount. Mohammed said that he would need time to gather up that much money. The lawyer teased him and said, "Why don't you ask your sugar momma for money?" I wanted to punch him in the throat. He had no idea what kind of salt he had just poured on a wounded man's ego. I hated him.

I knew how badly Mohammed wanted this change. He was so helpful to me when I needed money to open SOS, so I wanted to do the same. I offered to loan him $80,000. But I was careful—very careful—about how I framed it. I knew how fragile his ego could be, especially when it came to money and his pride as a doctor. I didn't want him to feel emasculated or resentful, so I made it clear that the loan was coming from my company, not from me personally. I even drafted paperwork to reflect that. It wasn't about control or power—it was about protecting our peace. I just wanted him to get what he wanted without making him feel small. I hoped that by presenting it this way, the loan wouldn't become a wedge between us.

He took some time to reflect and then quietly accepted my offer. I was happy to have his approval. It seemed like he treated me better for the next few weeks. I began to see a light at the end of the dark tunnel.

At the time, we were renting a house. But after everything I had accomplished—finally making real money—I wanted to reward myself. I had this dream. I wanted to build us a home. Not just a house but a real family home. Something stable. Something permanent. Moving would be like a fresh start. Maybe a new shiny space would help with all the tension. Now, as a teenager, I wanted Meez to have a bigger closet. I wanted a bigger garage for all of Mohammed's cars. I thought that would make him happy.

So I started looking for empty lots, but it had to be in Meez's school district. That was non-negotiable. She had already been through so much change I wasn't going to pull her away from the one place she had stability. But the area was expensive—everywhere I looked was far outside my budget.

And then, like a gift, the lot directly across from Meez's high school had a for sale sign. I imagined how awesome it would be for Meez to walk to school! It was being sold by an old man now in assisted living with no children, no heirs, just a patch of land he was ready to let go of for almost nothing. It felt like divine timing. I was so excited—I talked to Mohammed about it, and he agreed. I swept it up right away.

I got started on the house plans and threw myself into it like it was my lifeline. I tried to bring Mohammed in. I wanted it to feel like *our* dream. I'd ask him questions: "Do you like this layout? How big should our bedroom be? Do you want one big master closet or his and hers?" And every time, he brushed me off.

One day, his brother and his wife came over to visit. I showed my sister-in-law my decor ideas like a proud child showing their mother a picture they drew. Mohammed looked over my Pinterest vision board. "I don't want to fight," he said in front of everyone. "Couples fight when they build houses. I trust you. I like your style. Whatever you pick is fine." It was the first attempt he had made to NOT argue with me. I was actually happy, thinking that he was starting to put effort into our marriage. So, I took him at his word.

I worked with the architect. I added a little shop space for him, thinking he could keep his car stuff there, maybe even build something of his own. I did everything I could to make it something he would love. When the first draft came back, I showed it to him—excited, hopeful. His face darkened. "Why didn't you consult me?" he snapped. "This is everything *you* want. You want this to be just YOUR house! You should have asked me."

And I just stood there, stunned. It was like living in a maze with no exits. He had *told* me not to involve him. But now I was being punished for doing exactly that. I showed him a draft—not the final plan. I was asking for his input. Everything I did was wrong. Nothing I did was right.

There was this one evening I remember so vividly. He got home from work, sat on the couch, opened his laptop, and started working. And I thought—okay. I'm going to be the one to try. I'll make the first move. Physical touch was always the love language for us both; maybe if I just sat beside him quietly and peacefully, it could help bridge the gap. No words, so nothing to start a fight.

So I did. I sat next to him, just to be close. My leg barely touched his. He turned and looked at me like I had completely invaded his space—like I was dirt under his shoe. A nuisance. He gave me a look I'll never forget. And then he stood up, walked over to the loveseat across from me, and sat there instead. It felt like a slap in the face. I got up quietly so he wouldn't see how much it hurt. I went upstairs and just crawled into bed.

Over and over again, it was the same thing. Eggshelled days, confusion, more gaslighting. Chastised for this, ignored for that. He never let me *feel* safe. Never let me feel loved. And still—I stayed.

I remember one time his phone lit up while it was lying on the table. It was instinct to look—your eyes just flick toward movement. And the second I glanced at it, he grabbed it and flipped it over like I was spying on him. Like I was the untrustworthy one. It wasn't just the possibility of ongoing infidelity that gutted me—it was the betrayal of trust, the quiet confirmation that I was no longer his person. What was he hiding? Were they laughing at me? Was he venting about me, exaggerating my flaws to justify whatever he was doing behind my back? The not knowing was almost worse than the truth. It made my heart ache in the kind of silence that only secrets create.

One day, he left his phone on the couch and went to the bathroom. And I don't know—maybe I shouldn't have, but I picked it up. I scrolled through his messages, expecting to find incriminating messages with another woman. However, I didn't find anything like that... but I did find big black holes.

Every single conversation with Meez's mother was gone. Not just bits and pieces—every single message had been deleted like they never existed. Wiped clean. This was very unusual. He normally kept all of her messages—just in case she tried to fight for custody. He would usually download them like records and keep them in a file on the computer.

It was obvious. He was definitely hiding something. I did not even consider the possibility that he was cheating with her—that would never happen. But maybe he was talking about me to her and didn't want me to read it.

I waited until he came back, and I asked him calmly, "Where are all the messages from Meez's mom?"

He shrugged. "I don't know."

"You deleted them," I said. "Why would you delete *everything*? Were you saying something about me you didn't want me to see?"

He just stood there, silent. No explanation. No denial. No apology. Just that infuriating blankness. So I said, "Whatever it is you're saying about me, I hope you can say it to *my face* so we can actually fix this. I feel so much animosity from you, and I don't think that I deserve it. What did I do to make you hate me so much?"

And I told him—I wanted marriage counseling. I told him something was broken between us, and I didn't want to give up on us. He flat-out refused. "No," he said. "I'm not doing that with you."

So I said, "Well, *I'm* going to sign up. And I hope you'll join me."

That night, I went upstairs alone. I lay there with the glow of the phone in my hand and signed up for a virtual marriage counselor. I picked appointment times that lined up with when he'd be home. Maybe if he heard it happening, he would decide to join.

I kept the door open during sessions and spoke loud enough so he could hear every word—what I was saying, what the counselor was saying. I told him that Mohammed had cheated on me. I told him that I didn't care who the other woman was—that I would forgive him. I wanted him to know I was fighting for us, that I was trying, and that I *wanted* this to work.

Session after session, I would tell the counselor about all the ways I was trying to reconnect with Mohammed. I tried holding his hand, made his favorite dinners, complimented him, supported him, and encouraged him. I walked on eggshells and danced around his moods. It was hard facing repeated rejection from the one who you love the most.

The marriage counselor encouraged me to keep trying. He gave me advice and ideas on how to reach him through this wall. I absorbed his every word and tried everything. I was finally able to hold a conversation with Mohammed about sex. It had been months since we had been intimate. He complained that I didn't initiate, and he felt unwanted—he believed that it was my fault. I told him that I understood and would try harder for him.

One evening, I walked past our master bathroom and found him standing naked after a shower. I lifted my eyebrows and told him how sexy he was. He was startled, bent his knees, and covered his bits. "Stop objectifying me!" he screamed as he slammed the door. *Well, that didn't get the reaction I hoped it would.*

A few weeks later, he told me he had a work trip coming up. He said it was a cardiology conference in Hawaii, and he needed the CEUs.

For a second—just a second—I got excited. I thought maybe it was a chance for us to reconnect. A change of scenery without the social pressure of having friends around. I asked, "Are we taking Meez with us?" He didn't even look up. "No," he said. "I'm going on a trip. Alone. I need you to stay with Meez. She can't miss school," even though he'd never had an issue pulling her out before.

I stared at him, swallowing back the hurt. "Oh. Ok." And that was that. Again. I had been trying so hard to be the perfect wife. Complimenting him, reacting positively to everything, and always being the one to adapt and smooth over the rough spots. Just doing everything I could to make him happy, to make it work.

And so, for those five days, I became a one-woman show. I packed her lunches, drove her to school, went to work, picked her up, and drove her back home. Meez and I had a great weekend, actually. We went shopping, and I bought her some new outfits to help her feel confident. We watched a movie and cooked dinner together.

Mohammed never called to check in on me while he was away. I heard Meez talking on her phone to someone in the evenings, so I assumed he called to check on her.

When Mohammed came home, everything fell apart. I was doing everything I could to be the perfect wife—when I opened his suitcase to wash his clothes, a half-empty bottle of Viagra fell out. I knew without a doubt he wasn't using that with me. The realization hit like a cold wave. He was STILL having an affair. It wasn't just a one-time fling. And now he was taking her on trips!?!

I had no idea how to approach this. He wasn't even trying to hide it anymore. He wanted me to start a fight. He wanted the explosion of emotion from me so that he could point at me and call me crazy.

I didn't want to start a fight, but I also couldn't pretend it didn't bother me. I didn't know how to handle this new reality. I was about to bring it up when he said, "I actually want to talk to you about something," he said.

"Okay. What do you want to talk about?" I dreaded what he was about to say.

"I need you to come with me to the title company on Wednesday. I bought a house, and you need to sign."

I froze. Bought a house? How could he have done that without even telling me? I had just got our house plans approved by the city and was about to pour the slab for our dream family home. I thought we were on the same page. How could he have bought a house behind my back?

"What house?" I asked, heart pounding. "Where is it? How big is it? What does it look like?"

His answer felt strange. "It's a small house, a townhouse," he said. "I know we're renting this place, and I know building a house is going to take a while. I don't want to keep renting, so I bought this townhouse. We can live in it until the new house is done, and then we can rent it out as an investment property."

His excuse did not make sense at all. Why buy a house when we were already about to build our family home? Why waste the money on something so temporary when we'd need to buy furniture and other things for the new house? If it really was an investment property, why would he hide this from me until the last minute? Why couldn't we have shopped for investment homes together?

And that's when it hit me, the full realization of what was happening. He was preparing to exit. He knew I was building this big house with the money I had made. He knew that if we divorced, I could claim it as mine, and he wanted to have somewhere to go… or maybe even somewhere to take another woman. I felt numb.

So, I asked him point blank. I had to know. "Are you leaving me for your whore?"

His reaction was immediate, an over-the-top denial. "Of course not. Why would you say that? Just because we're having problems doesn't mean I'm cheating. Why would you accuse me of that? I would never…" It was a performance. The kind of overreaction that only confirmed what I already suspected—he was lying.

Then, I pointed to the Viagra bottle, which was still on the floor next to the suitcase. "Who were you with in Hawaii? You never go anywhere by yourself. Are you really choosing another woman over me? After everything I've done for this family? After building us a home? After starting a business for Meez?"

He became very angry and spit words into my face, "You should be GRATEFUL that I allowed you the opportunity to help raise my child." I was shocked at how much hate came out of his mouth.

He continued to deny cheating, of course. Over and over again, but I had had enough. I called the contractor. I told them to cancel the construction on the house. I told them I wasn't moving forward with it. Even though the plans had been approved by the city and everything was in motion, I couldn't bear the thought of living in that house by myself, so I trashed the plans.

That was the moment when I stopped trying.

I started doing a little house shopping myself. I found one nearby, within walking distance of the townhouse he had bought. I was going to make him choose—me or her. I wasn't so full of myself to think that I was irreplaceable…but I was confident enough to know that if he did replace me, it would be a downgrade. Who else could this man pull who would be prettier than me? Younger than me? More independent than me? As faithful as me?

I sat him down, my heart heavy, and I said, "I want to move out. I think it's time for a trial separation. Clearly, everything I do annoys you. Every time I breathe, it irritates you. You, evidently, want to be with someone else. So I think a separation is the best thing for both of us. And honestly, when I leave, I hope you miss me. I hope you realize what you've lost. Maybe then, you'll come back, ask me on a date, and we can figure out what comes next. But I can't stay here anymore. I can't live in this house with you hating me like this. It's killing me."

I thought maybe he would break down. Maybe he would be upset or regretful, ask me to stay, and ask to join the counseling sessions. Maybe he would fight for us… but none of that happened.

His face was completely neutral. It was as if nothing I said registered at all. The only thing he could muster was, "Well, if you want to go, I can't stop you."

My mind went blank. I felt nothing. The numbness swept over me, and I felt completely detached. I felt like a third person in the corner of the room, watching me sitting there next to him, being rejected for the last time.

He finally broke the silence, "From now on, I want you to sleep in the spare bedroom. You can stay here until you find a new place to go."

It was laughable, really. He hadn't slept in the same room as me for months. But now, he wanted to punish me. He wanted to show me that this was happening, that I was the one initiating a breakup. It felt like a cruel game, but it wasn't a game for me. It was my life, and I was done.

I took my stuff and went into the spare bedroom, and every day, I would wake up, get dressed, go to work, pick Meez up from school, go back home, feed us dinner, and just go into my room and shut the door. Every evening, I secretly hoped that when he would come home, he would knock on my door and talk to me, but it never happened.

The next time he talked to me was about a week later when he said he was going on another trip. He didn't tell me where but asked me again to watch Meez. He said it was just a weekend trip—he would be back on Monday evening. I obviously agreed to it. "Of course. I'll do anything for her."

Meez and I had an uneventful weekend. We went to a pottery painting place and ate pizza at a new restaurant. Sunday night, I was scrolling through YouTube when a new music video came across my feed. It was "Traitor" by Olivia Rodrigo. My emotions finally came out. I cried. I was angry. I didn't deserve any of this. Who the hell was he with? I wanted to lash out at him... so I posted that YouTube link on his Facebook page. I got no response.

That Monday was a big day for me. I had a potential franchisee from Phoenix flying into Houston to take a tour of the corporate office, meet with me, and talk numbers. I was very excited to meet with these people. The idea of a SOS opening in a new state was huge. So I dressed really nicely, put on good makeup, dropped Meez off at school, and drove to the office. I met with the two well-dressed men, shook hands like a confident businesswoman, and started giving them a tour. While we walked around, I explained what each room was for and how they were designed to be sensory-friendly. I explained everything that SOS does to help the kids learn in a good environment.

I felt my phone vibrate in my pocket. I glanced down to read Mohammed's text. "I want you out by this evening. I saw what you did on Facebook, evidently."

It was like a slap in the face, delivered coldly, without any warning, without any consideration for the years we had spent together. I tried so hard not to show any reaction, but one of my employees noticed. She said I looked suddenly white, like I might pass out at any moment. She immediately pulled me into another room, away from the potential franchises, and asked me what had happened. I showed her the message, and I could feel the tears start welling up in my eyes. I tried to blink them away.

"Oh my God," she whispered. "It's going to be okay. Maybe he didn't mean it that way. Maybe the text was for someone else."

But I knew better. I had no doubt about the meaning behind those words. I felt the weight of everything coming to a head, and before I knew it, the tears came rushing out. I couldn't hold it in anymore. I cried, not just from the betrayal but from the overwhelming realization that everything I had worked so hard to build—the family, the business, the future—was collapsing.

She hugged me, trying to reassure me, and then said, "I've got this. I'll finish the tour with them. You go take care of what you need to."

I was grateful for her support because I couldn't focus on anything else. I refused to let Mohammed see me broken. I knew what he wanted. He wanted me to react, to be the bad guy. But I wasn't going to do that. I couldn't let Meez see me in that state, either. I wanted her to stay in her safe little world for as long as possible.

So, I did what I had to do. I took a deep breath, gathered my mental strength, and called two of my male employees. I told them what was happening, and we drove to the house. We didn't waste any time. We packed up everything I could take as fast as we could, and we loaded it all into a storage unit. By the time Mohammed came home that evening, my things were gone. There would be no confrontation. No drama. Just silence. He had made his decision, and I had walked away.

Now, the next problem—where would I go? I was officially homeless. I remembered an episode of House MD where the main character advised his friend, "As long as you are in a hotel, it's temporary, which means it's still just a fight. But if you get a permanent place to stay, it's a breakup." So I decided to move into a hotel for the time being, but my friend, Taylor, was absolutely against this idea.

Taylor opened her doors, her arms, and her heart to me without hesitation. She bought a bed and a little dresser and made a bedroom for me out of her home office. Her kindness reminded me that love didn't always have to come with conditions, cold stares, or cruel silence. At Taylor's, I was wanted. I was seen. Every morning, before the sun got too hot, Taylor and I would walk our dogs together, coffee in hand, talking about everything and nothing. Every evening, I came home from work to a warm meal, to laughter, to the sound of our dogs playing in the backyard together. We would talk about our day and laugh at each other's stories.

On weekends, we went to the bay. Her boyfriend taught me to ride a stand-up jet ski. After our legs were too weak to go further, we would pack up and stop for pizza on the way home. There was no animosity. No tip-toeing. No tension.

I felt something I hadn't felt in a long time: safety. It's crazy how much abuse I had learned to live through… like a frog in a pot, not realizing how hot it was becoming. Now that I was out, I felt like I could breathe. I hadn't even realized that I was holding my breath. I started to remember who I was. It was like the fog of gaslighting and confusion was finally lifting. I hadn't realized how deeply I had been buried in that darkness until I stepped into the light.

But, of course, the reality of divorce was still lurking in my head. That Friday, I got the text: "I already filed for divorce. Give me your address so you can be served. And I'm not going to reimburse you the $80,000. I don't think that I should have to pay back the company that I helped get off the ground."

Just like that. Cold. Businesslike. No conversation. No closure. And yet, I wasn't shocked. I think deep down, I knew that this had been his endgame all along. He got what he wanted, and now he had no use to keep me around. He would be on to his next victim.

That afternoon, Mohammed posted on his Facebook page, **"This Thanksgiving season, I want to be thankful for my family, my kids, and my friends. Sadly, my marriage ended when Nichole told me she was buying her own house to live alone, away from Meez and me. As it is not the family life I would have imagined, I had no choice but to file for divorce. Be good to the people in your life. And tell them you love them often. You never know when the life you thought you had is taken away."**

What a dick.

Hilariously, when his first wife (Lilo's mom) saw that post, she called me. She asked what happened and apologized on his behalf. She admitted to speaking with him first. He told her that he never loved me. He said that I had manipulated him into asking me to move in. He said that I bought the ring and planned the wedding like a freight train that couldn't be stopped. He played the victim.

Lilo's mom is a psychiatrist—she didn't buy his story. She said that he was stupid for letting me go, that he couldn't expect to find anyone better. She asked if I needed a place to stay and offered to give me Lilo's old room since she moved away for college. Could you imagine? Us living together? Like the ex-wives club? It made me laugh. She was so kind to me.

It was then that we both realized that I had been together with him for eight years. I should have listened to him when he told me that his life moved in 8-year cycles when we were dating. It was just another 8-year adventure for him.

Lilo's mom explained to me what Love Bombing is—a tool that narcissists use to get what they want as fast as possible. And once they no longer find use of you, they leave abruptly. They aren't affected by the break up because there was never any real connection for them. It opened my eyes to so much.

I went back to my real estate agent, and I said, let's get that house that I liked. She discouraged me and said it was way overpriced, but it was the only thing I liked that was for sale close to Meez. I made an offer, and they accepted, but it took a while to close. So, I was homeless for six weeks.

Once the house was mine, Taylor was actually upset and tried to convince me to stay with her. I wasn't excited about living alone either, but I wanted to be close to Meez.

I texted Mohammed my new address and offered to continue picking up Meez from school in the afternoons. He replied, "Well, then your plight of homelessness is over. Congrats! You have got all you wanted. Nuclear Tech to a self-made woman! What a journey! You're rich, famous, and adored by everyone. I would very much like to never hear from you again. Please enjoy the rest of your life as if you never knew me."

That's when the real heartbreak started to unfold. He started gatekeeping our daughter. I wasn't allowed to pick her up from school anymore. Everything had to be coordinated through him. I had to ask permission to spend time with her, and he would say yes sometimes, but I always knew why. It was convenient. When she was with me, he was free to do whatever—or whomever—he wanted.

I didn't care. I'd take crumbs of time with her over none. I would text her, I would call her, I would offer to pick her up from school, take her to dinner, help with homework, or just sit with her and talk. Lilo and Meez both spent a day with me just before Christmas. We made cookies together and did a huge jigsaw puzzle. It was so special.

But over time, Meez stopped answering my texts. At first, I thought maybe her phone had died or she was busy. But then the calls stopped going through. Texts weren't being read. I knew what that meant—I had been blocked. Silence. Like a switch had flipped. I knew he had said something— something to poison her against me. I could feel it. And just like that, I lost my daughter. It shattered me.

Even knowing that I was blocked, every Monday, without fail, I sent her a message—just in case she decided to look. I sent them for two years. Two years of Mondays. I told her I loved her. I told her about my day. I told her I missed her and that I was always here. And then, one Monday, I just... stopped.

I had gone through every stage of grief. Anger. Bargaining. Depression. Denial. Over and over until finally, I told myself, you have to stop waiting. You have to stop hoping. She's gone. She believes whatever version of me he painted in her mind, and I'm not sure she'll ever come back from that.

So, I poured myself into SOS. It was the only thing I had left. I always felt like my success had a cost—and I had already paid in full with my home, marriage, and daughter. So I thought, fine. If I've already lost everything else, I might as well win this.

Chapter 12: The Journey Continues

I worked harder than I ever had in my life. Sometimes 14-hour days. I revamped the 300-page operations manual. I took marketing classes and leadership workshops, networked with professionals, and made appearances on every podcast I could find. I pushed through exhaustion, heartbreak, and grief. I pushed through silence and loneliness.

Even though I was happy, I walked through the world guarded, half-trusting. Life, after all, had been less than kind. It had taught me to expect abandonment, disappointment, and silence.

I experienced more grief along the way. Employees that I helped turned against me. Others left bad reviews or quit without notice. I was sued more times than I can count, mostly for ridiculous reasons. I paid for more billing mistakes. Every appliance I bought for the office seemed to break… but nothing worth doing is ever easy.

Juliet got married and welcomed a beautiful baby girl into the world. Kendra walked down the aisle not long after. It felt as if we grew up together, sisters in spirit, bound by shared dreams and seasons of life. There was a comforting rhythm to it all. For the first time in a long time, I felt peace.

My training team produced a wealth of training materials, including videos, to help franchisees absorb all the information quickly. My marketing team developed premade ads—both video and picture formats—that franchisees could use to promote their own clinics. We now had tangible assets to offer new franchisees, making our model even more attractive. We improved our website and created practice management software.

SOS Franchising was in a stronger position than ever before. Joe and I started attending franchise expos, where we showcased our business model. With COVID in the rearview mirror, we had something new to offer in our sales pitch—a recession-proof business model. The response was overwhelmingly positive. In 2021, Joe sold a total of 18 territories.

In 2022, we sold 12 more territories and opened clinics in new states. *Success on the Spectrum* won the "Health 2.0 – Outstanding Organization" Award from the International Forum in Advancements in Healthcare. I was so proud. I hung the plaque in the lobby. Collectively, SOS centers made over $8 million dollars.

In 2023, we sold 20 more territories. I had to double the size of our training and support team to keep up. I promoted Juliet to Director of Onboarding and hired staff underneath her to help all the new CEOs start their own clinics. I could hardly believe that we made over $21 million dollars that year.

In 2024, we sold a massive 38 territories. We felt like heroes. I traveled to each grand opening. City after city, I shook hands with mayors and cut more ribbons than I could count. I practically lived out of my suitcase. In July, the city of Houston awarded me with the Houston Humanitarian Award at a black-tie event that was televised live on the news. It was a dream come true. By the end of the year, we collectively made just under $40 million dollars.

I felt so happy and light... and as they say, love comes knocking when you stop looking for it. I guess fate had a sense of humor because it led me straight into the arms of a man from Louisiana. He, too, had escaped the confines of a small town in pursuit of a bigger life. And so I remarried— to this glorious man who doesn't punish me for being powerful, who doesn't weaponize silence, who isn't threatened by a woman who makes more money than him. A man who loves me gently, fully, and steadily.

In March 2025, we were awarded our 100th territory. It was a milestone I could hardly believe. From those humble beginnings in that first ghetto-fabulous office to building a national franchise, we had grown into a community—a network of people who had the same mission. People didn't see the company as mine but as OURS. These brave franchisees chose to pick up the same torch as me—to help the kids.

The heartwarming part is that twenty-five percent of SOS CEOs are autism parents—warriors in their own right—who know the journey not by map but by muscle memory. They are not business people by trade. They are architects of miracles.

Together, we have not just formed a business. We built something that has helped thousands of families. We have rewritten the narrative that autism parents are handed—one of grief and limits—and turned it into a story of growth. I've come to understand that when you help a child with autism, you are not just teaching them to speak or play or sit still for five more minutes. You are helping a family breathe again. You are unclenching fists that have been tight for years. You are handing them back their futures.

And the feeling of knowing—truly knowing—that the company I built changes lives? That is the flame that keeps me warm in the coldest hours. The impact—it is almost too large to cup in human hands.

I am amazingly proud. But not in the chest-pounding way of ego. It's a quieter pride. The kind that shows up when I hear a child speak for the first time. When a mother calls crying because her son said, "I love you," for the first time. When a father no longer has to fear for his child's future. That's what we did. That's what we do.

Sometimes, I catch myself in the mirror and think—did I really do this? The feeling is surreal as if I had stepped into someone else's movie. Imposter syndrome, they call it. But then I remember: no, this is mine. I walked through fire for this. I bled for this.

In the end, I have come to understand that my true destiny was never to be Mohammad's wife. I once believed he was the purpose, the finish line, the reason behind it all. He was simply the catalyst, the stepping stone that I needed to create SOS. It was through the pain, the lessons, and the resilience that I discovered my real calling: to build a company that would change lives across the country. Helping families navigate autism offers hope where there was once despair—that was always my path. And I wouldn't trade that destiny for anything.

It is clear that the hard work, the sacrifices, the moments of doubt, and the leaps of faith have all been worth it. My mission remains steady, and the structure we have worked so hard to build has grown in ways I couldn't have predicted.

What I have learned through all of this is that success always comes with sacrifice. I hope that as you turned these pages, you found pieces of your own journey reflected in mine. Let this be your reminder that hard times are not the end—they're just part of the climb. Doubt may whisper in your ear, and naysayers may try to dim your light, but your truth is your power.

Keep going. Build something meaningful. Love fearlessly. And when your time is done, let the world bear witness that you were here—and that it is better because of you.